Reminisce Life in AMERiCA

CELEBRATING THE SPIRIT OF OUR COUNTRY

table of contents

page 18

page 43

page 27

page 100

REMINISCE LIFE IN AMERICA
Catherine Cassidy **Vice President, Editor-in-Chief**
Heidi Reuter Lloyd **Vice President, Executive Editor/Books**
Mark Hagen **Sr. Editor/Books**
Michelle Rozumalski **Editor**
Ellie Martin Cliffe **Associate Editor**
Edwin Robles Jr. **Associate Creative Director**
Raeann Sundholm **Art Director**
Julie Wagner **Content Production Manager**
Kathy Crawford, Catherine Fletcher **Layout Designers**
Deb Warlaumont Mulvey **Copy Chief**
Joanne Weintraub **Copy Editor**
Jean Dal Porto **Project Proofreader**
Trudi Bellin **Photo Coordinator**
Mary Ann Koebernik **Assistant Photo Coordinator**
Barb Czysz **Administrative Assistant**

Heather Lamb **Executive Editor, Home & Garden**
Sharon K. Nelson **Creative Director, Home & Garden**
John Burlingham **Sr. Editor, *Reminisce***
Cheryl A. Michalek **Art Director, *Reminisce***
Blanche Comiskey **Editorial Assistant, *Reminisce***

Lisa Karpinski **Vice President, General Manager, RD Milwaukee**
Dan Fink **Vice President/Book Marketing**
Jim Palmen **Creative Director/Creative Marketing**

THE READER'S DIGEST ASSOCIATION, INC.
Robert E. Guth **President and Chief Executive Officer**
Dan Lagani **President, North America**

REMINISCE BOOKS
©2012 Reiman Media Group, LLC
5400 S. 60th St., Greendale WI 53129-1404

International Standard Book Number (10): 1-61765-001-3
International Standard Book Number (13): 978-1-61765-001-7

Library of Congress Control Number: 2011938022
All rights reserved. Printed in U.S.A.

For additional copies of this book or information on other books, write:
Reminisce Customer Care
P.O. Box 5294
Harlan IA 53593-0794
Call toll-free: 800-344-6913

Visit our website at *reminisce.com*

"As American as apple pie…"

You've probably heard that expression before. It's the perfect description for this all-new, one-of-a-kind book from America's No. 1 nostalgia magazine.

From cover to cover, *Reminisce: Life in America* celebrates our unique experiences in the great country we call home. This special collection features nine big chapters packed with heartwarming, humorous memories and personal photos shared by *Reminisce* magazine readers from around the nation.

Feel your heart swell with star-spangled spirit when you read about the generous townspeople who fed hungry World War II troops traveling by train—the story is on page 18 in the "Patriotic Pride" chapter. Turn to page 30 in "From Sea to Shining Sea," and you'll get a bird's-eye view of Mount Rushmore from a reader whose father helped carve its monumental faces.

America's never-give-up attitude is on full display in a Kansas family's recollection of surviving the Dust Bowl, featured on page 56 in "We Can Do It." On page 82 in "The American Dream," you're sure to be moved by the story of an immigrant who reconnected with his 99-year-old mother in the old country.

Helping on the home front is highlighted in an Oregon native's account of welding Liberty ships—you'll find it on page 112 in "Hard at Work." And see page 124 in "Family Values" for the Christmas lesson an Indiana woman will never forget.

There's plenty of fun to be had on page 142 in "That's Entertainment," where you'll share the excitement of a Florida mom who met the legendary Elvis Presley. Then travel to Weyers Cave, Virginia, on page 178 in "Small Town, Big City" for the reflections of Southerners who welcomed a New York boy into their home and hearts.

"The Spirit of Youth" showcases America's younger generations, including a Georgia farm girl who didn't back down in the face of an arm-wrestling challenge. You're sure to chuckle at this side-splitting tale on page 187.

What's more, this can't-miss book includes a bonus journal section on pages 206-208. Simply jot down memories of your own American experiences to turn this treasury into a personalized keepsake for loved ones.

We hope you enjoy reminiscing as you enjoy the many memories and photos in this book—all different, but all telling one unique story: the story of America.

Best to you all,
The editors of *Reminisce* magazine

Patriotic PRIDE

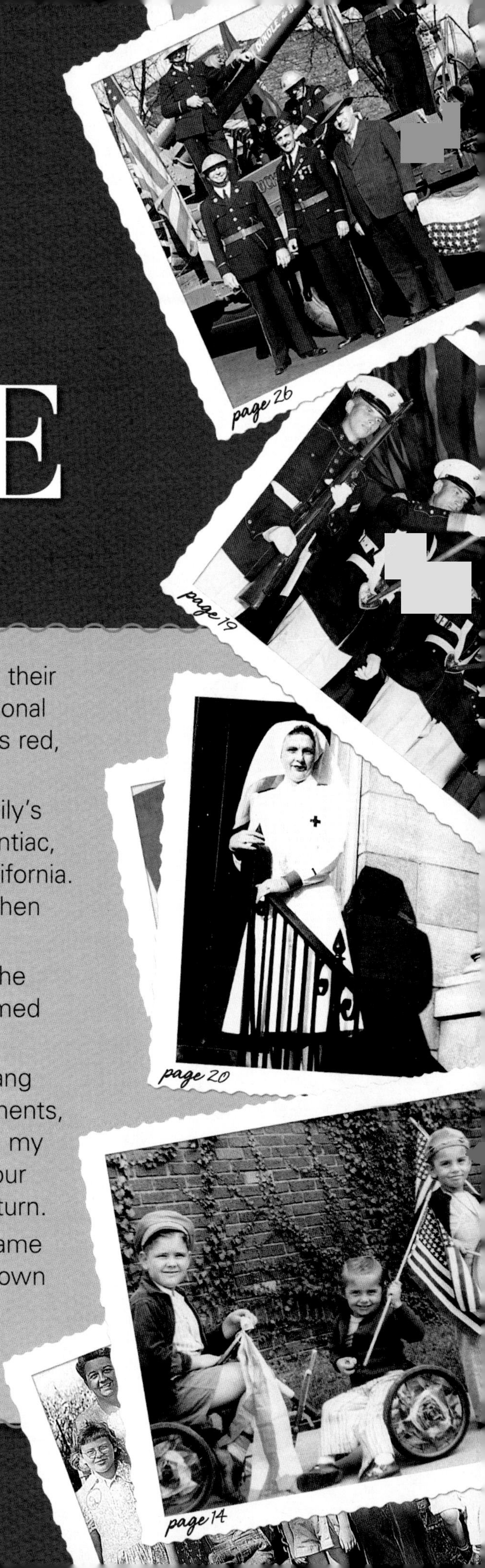

O say, can you see…the love Americans have for their country? Throughout our nation's history, inspirational events and flag-waving occasions have colored us red, white and blue.

"When I was a teen, I played piano for our family's weekly sing-along parties held at our home in Pontiac, Michigan," says Jeanne Cartier of Springville, California. "Our lives drastically changed on Dec. 7, 1941, when the Japanese attacked Pearl Harbor.

"One by one, my five older brothers all joined the service. Our weekly house parties were transformed into gatherings of servicemen and their girls.

"We all became part of one large family that sang together, celebrated milestones such as engagements, and helped each other through hard times. When my brother Bob went missing in action in Germany, our songs turned sacred as we prayed for his safe return.

"Eventually and miraculously, all my brothers came home. We sang ballads of peace as we settled down to live in a more tranquil world."

This chapter serves as a star-spangled salute to Americans' enduring spirit of patriotism.

page 26

page 19

page 20

page 14

Seeds of VICTORY

THIS GARDEN HARVEST INCLUDED A BOUNTIFUL SENSE OF PRIDE.

By Gladys Winterrowd, Oblong, Illinois

Down the cinder lane and into our house I ran, barely noticing the wood-framed screen door banging shut behind me.

"Mom, Mom, look!" I cried as I caught my breath. "Seeds! My own seeds! Can I have my own garden, Mom? Can I?"

"May I," my mother corrected me, closing the door to the oven of our large, wood-burning range and wiping her forehead with the hem of her apron.

I spread the tiny packets of seeds from my schoolteacher onto the red-and-white checkered oilcloth covering the kitchen table. The plain brown government-issue envelopes were about 2 by 3 inches with black lettering.

They weren't pretty, like the seed packages in the store—the glossy ones with colorful pictures of white-tipped red-globe radishes or bright orange carrots. But they were all mine.

It was the spring of 1945, the waning months of a long world war of which I was vaguely aware in rural Douglas County, Illinois. My one brother, Clarence, 12 years older than I, was no longer at the supper table each evening. He appeared at home from time to time, tall and handsome in a Navy uniform, to sweep me off my feet and twirl me around.

"These seeds are for your victory garden," Mother said, explaining that it took a lot of food to feed all of our sailors and soldiers and that the President wanted everyone to grow their own food to save more for the war.

Mother said that while we didn't have a place to create my own separate garden, I could plant my seeds at the ends of a couple of rows in the big garden.

I piped up that I wanted my own garden, but Mother said, "Don't be putting up a tune. Your daddy has enough on his mind without worrying about making you a garden."

A few afternoons later, I heard Mother calling to me as I skipped up the narrow road from school, my metal dinner bucket swinging and bumping against my legs.

THE GOOD EARTH. This circa-1945 photo shows the author's mother, Audrey Halterman, working in the family's victory garden at their Illinois home.

There, between the garden ditch and fence, was a small rectangle of freshly turned earth, the clods broken up and the soil raked smooth for planting.

"Here is your victory garden," Mother said. "Daddy spaded it up for you at noon."

Each day, under Mother's watchful eyes, I pulled weeds and thinned the carrots and beets. "These are from Gladys' garden," Mother announced on the evening that my first radishes were served at the table with dinner. I glowed with pride.

In August, I was with Mother in the garden late one afternoon when the 6 o'clock whistle in town, about a mile away, blew early. Then came an eruption of sirens, car horns and church bells.

My older sister ran out of the house and called

out something, and Mother flung her hoe to the ground and clasped her rough, red hands to her breast, bursting into tears.

"What's wrong?" I cried, alarmed. "Mommy! What's wrong?"

"The war is over!" she said as she wept.

"If the war is over," I asked, "then why are you crying?"

"Because," she said with relief through her tears, "Clarence will be coming home."

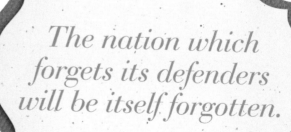

The nation which forgets its defenders will be itself forgotten.

—Calvin Coolidge

FAMILY TIES

JUST LIKE DAD. "When the fighting ended in Europe after World War II, my sister joined her husband, who was stationed in Germany," relates Marie Radeck of Silver Bay, Minnesota. "Helen bought a piece of the same fine woolen material that was used to make officers' shirts. She sent it to me, and I made a 'soldier suit' for our 3-year-old son, Hermie. His daddy was stationed in Italy during the war."

DESIRE TO SERVE. "This cherished family photo shows my grandmother with two of her sons," says Libby Phillips Peters of McDermott, Ohio. "My father, Willis Phillips, is seated, and his brother Stanley is in uniform. Uncle Stanley served in France during World War I. My dad was very unhappy that he was too young to join his brother in the service."

On Parade!

PULLED TOGETHER

Growing up in the city of St. Joseph, Missouri, we kids were always anxious for the annual apple blossom parade festival. From the carnival rides to bands that came from surrounding counties, it was an exciting event.

My buddy, Wayne Bottoroff, and I made up our minds to be a part of the next parade festival. Because our country was firmly entrenched in World War II, we decided that a victory garden would be a great idea. But how could we create one as a parade float?

Then we hit on the answer—an old radio flyer wagon. It would make the perfect container for our victory garden, and even better, we could easily pull it as we walked in the parade.

To dress the part, we donned overalls and straw hats. With a few garden tools and a little red-white-and-blue trim, we were all set.

When the big event finally arrived, we took our place in the parade lineup. It wasn't long before we discovered that walking in a parade takes a lot more energy than watching one.

Pulling the wagon in the hot, muggy weather, Wayne and I kept eyeballing each other as the parade stretched on for miles and hours. We each wondered how we both were able to convince each other that this was a good idea.

By the time the parade ended, the sweat was running off our noses. We didn't even know if we could make it back home without our parents rescuing us during the attempt.

Then we got the biggest surprise of all. Our little float had won first prize in the parade!

After receiving that honor, we didn't need anyone to take us home. We held our sweaty little noses high and proudly hauled our prizewinner all the way.

—Jim Jennings, St. Joseph, Missouri

NUMBER ONE. Jim Jennings (left) and pal Wayne Bottoroff had a challenging but rewarding time pulling their patriotic float in a community parade during World War II.

GRAND BAND. "My family always looked forward to the Hammond, Indiana, Memorial Day parade," writes Frances Sabo from Springfield, Illinois. "The photo of the Thomas A. Edison Elementary School marching band in 1960 (below) shows my brother, Jan Kocman, on the far right. In the photo taken before the parade, Jan is on the left, standing next to our brother Marty."

STARS AND STRIPES. "We were in all of the parades promoting the war effort in the 12th Ward of Allentown, Pennsylvania," writes Shirley Pozzi, who now lives in Center Valley. "The parades started at the fairgrounds, and we marched down Hamilton Street. I'm the nurse; my name was Shirley Niblick then. Pictured, from left, are Nancy Kranch, Betty Lichtenwalner, Chuck Lichtenwalner, Jack Ohl (in the wagon), me, Charley (as Uncle Sam), Dolly Rusch and Raymond Brown."

MARCHING ON. "This early-1940s photo, taken by my father, Gerald Haywood, shows a Fourth of July parade headed down Ashfield Street toward the bridge connecting the small town of Piedmont, West Virginia, with Westernport, Maryland," relates Richard Haywood of Laurel, Maryland. "There was always a big turnout for the parade, both in spectators and in marching bands that agreed to perform—usually from Maryland, West Virginia and Pennsylvania."

LET'S GO! If you can't find a parade, why not make your own? In this 1946 photo, patriotic youngsters in Pontiac, Michigan, were ready to celebrate the Fourth of July with drums and Old Glory. "My brother, Bill Hannan, is on the far left, and my other brother, Mike Hannan, is on the far right, next to me," says Mary Kay Gallagher of Moline, Illinois. "A friend, Bill Hill, is the other little boy."

Fireworks Raised Spirits

By Lou Gros Louis, Leesburg, Virginia

Every Fourth of July brings back memories of a time when my father brought our town together in a small but spectacular way.

During the 1940s, the population of Wilton, New Hampshire, was around 1,200. Our little community had seen 252 men and women leave home and go off to serve in World War II.

Dad, who was not eligible to enter the military, was looked upon as a town leader. As such, he wanted to boost the morale of those left behind, who feared for their parents, husbands, wives, sons, daughters, friends and other loved ones in harm's way.

To create diversions from their daily worries and struggles, my father organized band concerts, movies shown at the town hall and talent shows. But perhaps the best-loved event was the community fireworks display he put on at our house each Independence Day.

Dad purchased whatever fireworks he could find for the show, which was held at the edge of our yard, bordering a large apple orchard. On the afternoon of July Fourth, he began setting up banquet tables borrowed from the town hall and brought out all of our chairs.

For an added touch, Dad set up his Sears, Roebuck and Co. record player on the lawn. The rousing patriotic music began at noon.

As evening approached, folks started arriving. Many walked more than four miles due to the gas shortage. They carried plates and bowls of food, which they placed on the tables for everyone to enjoy.

When night fell, the show started. Dad lit skyrockets, Roman candles, lawn displays and loud boomers that drew enthusiastic applause from the gathered townspeople. Sometimes rockets sparked small fires where they landed, but we didn't worry. The town's two fire trucks were on hand to put them out.

All of us feasted on the potluck food as we watched the colorful bursts of light Dad sent into the sky. Eventually, he ran out of fireworks, and the show had to come to a close.

But the evening didn't end there. Before leaving, those of us in the crowd joined together in a patriotic gesture of our own.

We sang our national anthem and "God Bless America," our voices ringing out with renewed resolve to face whatever challenges lay ahead.

our time with
TRUMAN

A CHANCE ENCOUNTER WITH THE FORMER PRESIDENT OF THE UNITED STATES
MADE A STRONG IMPRESSION ON KIDS AND ADULTS ALIKE.

By Burton Hale, San Diego, California

I took my seventh-grade class from William Cullen Bryant Elementary School, in Kansas City, Missouri, on a field trip in April 1953. We traveled by train to the state capitol, in Jefferson City, but the highlight occurred on the way home.

One of the chaperones, Mrs. John Oliver, informed me that former President Harry S. Truman was aboard the train in one of the forward staterooms, and he had agreed to come back to our car and visit with the students.

Mrs. Oliver and I sat in the front seat of the car, awaiting his arrival. Ten minutes later, I looked up, and there stood the man who just 3 months earlier had been the leader of the free world.

There were no military bands playing, no Secret Service agents attending and no politicians tagging behind. A small man in a double-breasted suit and thick eyeglasses stood there with a big grin on his face.

After introductions, Mrs. Oliver left the two of us sitting together in the front seat while she hurried to the next car to bring other chaperones to meet Mr. Truman.

I felt rather tongue-tied. What could I say to the man who had conferred with world

"A Service Institution"

MISSOURI PACIFIC LINES

Harry Truman

leaders like Roosevelt, Churchill, Stalin, Eisenhower, the Pope and many others?

Knowing that there were 30 12-year-olds behind us trying to hear what we were saying didn't help either!

Mr. Truman soon put me at ease, chatting and asking me about my students, family and service in the Navy.

After the other chaperones were introduced, the President made his way down the aisle and greeted each student with a handshake, a few pleasant words and a big smile. Then he waited patiently while every student with a camera had their picture taken shaking hands with him. He never once lost his big grin.

After he left the car, I began tearing off sheets of the Missouri Pacific Railroad note pad Mr. Truman had handed me minutes earlier. He had taken the time to sign his autograph on each of the 40 sheets in the pad. So I passed out one to every student and chaperone. And I have that small scrap of paper to this day.

As the train pulled into the station at Independence, where the Trumans lived, it was raining and nearly dark. The kids opened the windows (Missouri Pacific still used such windows back then) and poked their heads out,

hoping to get one more glimpse of Mr. Truman as he left the train.

No one was there to meet him or carry his luggage. We saw him step down from the train, put on his big, brown felt hat, grab his luggage and take a detour toward our car, where 30 children and their chaperones were cheering and yelling good-byes.

He stopped near our train car, put down his luggage, removed his hat and stood there in the drizzling rain waving to our group.

Those 30 youngsters are now all adults of retirement age. And I'll bet not one of them has ever forgotten our meeting with the man in the double-breasted suit and big felt hat, who today is considered by most Americans to be among our nation's 10 greatest presidents.

Food for the Troops

It was May 29, 1943, and I was a 20-year-old Navy WAVE on a train going from New York to Norman, Oklahoma.

I was about to begin training as an Aviation Machinist Mate at the Naval Air Technical Training Center. Many other troops were on the same train, heading for parts unknown.

Our train was having great difficulty getting over the mountains because of its length. The engineer finally decided the crew must detach both the baggage and dining cars, which left us without food.

By the time we reached the next little town, it was Sunday, May 30—Memorial Day. When we pulled into the station, we were greeted by the most wonderful sight.

A large crowd was waiting for us on the platform. As it turned out, the engineer had radioed ahead and explained our predicament.

The townspeople had announced the news at all of their church services. Everyone went home and brought their Sunday dinners to the station to feed the hungry troops.

When I realized what these generous people had done for us, I cried. I was filled with pride for this town, its residents and America.

We got underway again, the troops well fed and excited. After arriving in Norman, we were busy settling into our new barracks and didn't have time to think about what had happened during the trip.

When I was finally able to reflect on that day, I couldn't remember the name of the town—something I've always regretted. I wish I could thank all those people for their kindness. They were our heroes. God bless them all!

—Helen Anderson Glass, Tucson, Arizona

> *Ask not what your country can do for you; ask what you can do for your country.*
>
> —John F. Kennedy

☆ On GUARD ☆

THE FEW, THE PROUD. In 1954, Cpl. John Johnson (far left) was a U.S. Marine stationed in Hawaii. "This photograph was taken at a Marine Corps birthday ball," he writes from Grand Rapids, Michigan. "Today, I'm a member of the Kent County Veterans Honor Guard. I guess the more things change, the more they stay the same."

TEEN SCENE. "My sister, lifelong girlfriends and I were members of the American Legion Auxiliary and served as the Legion's color guard for years," says Lillian Sherman Ross of Punta Gorda, Florida. "This 1947 Memorial Day photo shows us as teenagers at a cemetery in Walden, New York. Pictured from left are Florence Peterson Fitzgerald, me, Rose Peterson Oliva and my sister, Jean Sherman Angeloni."

the RED CROSS

MODEL CHILD. "As a young girl during World War I, my mother, Dorothy Byrne-Ehrenberg, posed for a Red Cross awareness campaign," relates Kurt Ehrenberg of Payson, Arizona. "Mom was born in 1910. This picture was taken by her grandfather, who ran a photography studio in Brooklyn, New York."

LADY IN WHITE. When Mary Ivey of Jackson, Tennessee, served as a Red Cross volunteer during World War II, she was required to wear a Red Cross uniform (left). Mary made the one she's wearing in the photo.

FIRST AID

Sure, I wave the American flag. Do you know a better flag to wave?

—John Wayne

dad's second stint

FATHER FOUGHT TO ENLIST AGAIN DURING WORLD WAR II—17 YEARS AFTER FIRST JOINING UP.

By Luella Knudsen, Batavia, Illinois

I'll never forget my father calling excitedly down the front stairs to my mother and me as we arrived home on that momentous December Sunday.

Mom and I had gone to church, where she sang in the choir, while Dad had stayed home to care for 10-month-old Baby Judy.

"Ella, Ella, they bombed Pearl Harbor! The Japanese bombed Pearl Harbor!"

Mom and I ran up the steps. The thought that something terrible must have happened ran through my 11-year-old mind. But yesterday had been a wonderful day, my birthday, and I felt very grown up. What could be wrong?

Breathlessly, Daddy stood in the doorway, holding Judy and motioning to the radio. The news reports were coming in fast, and the message was loud and clear: "This morning, at 8 a.m. Honolulu time, the Japanese—"

My dad, Watt Jachim, had proudly served in the Navy in 1924 (shown in the photo above left), when he was only 17. His mother, Grandma Jane,

had signed for him even though she knew he had to lie about his age to enlist. After completing boot camp at Great Lakes Naval Station in Northern Illinois, Dad was stationed at Pearl Harbor as a deep-sea diver.

But Grandma Jane soon began to have second thoughts. Worried about the danger her young son might face, she notified the Navy about Dad's true age and insisted they send him home.

Dad didn't want to leave, later recalling that, "Three times, the Navy threw my seabag off the ship, and three times I tossed it back onboard."

Eventually, Dad realized he had to accept the Navy's decision. Back at home, he met my mother, got married and started a family in Chicago.

Compelled to Enlist

Having served in Pearl Harbor 17 years earlier, the news about the bombing affected Dad deeply. We pored over newspaper articles and listened to radio broadcasts, hoping to get some good news, but there was none.

American troops were being bombed, killed and captured. At sea, the Navy was tormented

by Nazi U-boats, which prevented Allied ships from getting through. England was barely holding on.

My Uncle Henry had been drafted during the summer and was one of the first to ship out to fight in the South Pacific. Dad's cousin Naomi was a front-line Army flight nurse.

Dad was beside himself. His service was needed now! Not able to just sit idly by, he felt compelled to join the fight for freedom.

Dad tried to re-enlist, but every Navy recruitment office turned him away. They told him he was too old, needed dental work and had too many dependents.

Plus, the allotment checks he would get wouldn't begin for three months. How would we pay our $30 monthly rent?

Finding a Way

Friends and family joined the discussion and offered Dad their help. Our kind landlord said he would never evict our family for unpaid rent. Grandma said she would go to the Navy office and swear under oath the validity of Dad's birth certificate. And our dentist agreed to fix Dad's teeth on credit.

My mother cringed at the thought of all this charity. But it couldn't be helped. She knew her husband had to join the war effort, so she bravely and quietly accepted the assistance.

In 1942, Dad re-enlisted in the Navy and went on to fight in many battles, including the Battle of Normandy. For about four years, Mom, Judy and I would see him when he was on leave. Finally, in 1946, he came home for good.

I am so grateful that my father returned safe and sound from his second stint in the service during World War II. Still, I can't help but wonder if our dentist, dear old Dr. Blair, ever got paid.

RE-UPPED. Wearing his Navy uniform during World War II, the author's father, Watt Jachim, is shown in the top photo with wife Ella (left) and the author and above with the author and her younger sister, Judy.

football with the soldiers

By Bruce Bailey, McDonough, Georgia

I learned to play football in the fall of 1944. The games I liked most were the touch football games the kids in our Atlanta neighborhood played in the street.

It was against the law to play in the street, of course, and sometimes policemen cruising by would send our group of 10- and 11-year-olds elsewhere. But there were few cars on the road during those days of gas rationing.

One day we were playing in front of my house when a bus pulled up to its nearby stop. Two soldiers stepped off and walked in our direction.

When they stopped to watch us, we all tried hard to put on a show. Passes were thrown a little farther, receivers jumped a little higher and, of course, mouths were a little louder.

The muscular blond sergeant and the tall corporal wearing glasses cheered our good plays, applauded valiant efforts and laughed at the sillier arguments. We were sorry when they eventually turned away and continued up the sidewalk, heading over the hill and out of sight.

But to our surprise and delight, they returned a short while later. We had moved to my backyard— on the advice of a policeman—and the soldiers asked if they could join our game.

Could they! Could Roy Rogers play cowboys with us?

It was great fun. The sergeant threw me a touchdown pass, then made me feel 10 feet tall when he said I'd made a good catch. We played for nearly an hour, and when we finally quit, the soldiers stayed for a while to talk.

The sergeant, Jack Bragger, was in town with the Third Air Force football team, the Gremlins. They were playing the Second Air Force Superbombers in the semifinal game of a series to determine the Air Force champs.

Jack played center and showed us how he snapped the ball. He shot it to the corporal, whose name we never did learn, so hard that it would have knocked one of us down. And he could snap the ball farther than any of us could pass it.

Jack also mentioned that Charley Trippi, a hero of the University of Georgia's 1943 Rose Bowl victory, was playing on his team.

None of us kids saw Jack and Charley's big Air Force game, played at Georgia Tech's Grant Field in December of 1944. But we learned their team won in an upset victory.

Charley had thrown two touchdowns in the game. He became an idol of mine and went on to play professional football for the Chicago Cardinals.

I don't know whether Jack had a hand in his team's victory or not. But to me, this soldier who had once played football with us kids was a legend all the same.

SONGS FOR AMERICA

When I was in the sixth grade in Amherst, Virginia, our country was fighting World War II. We showed our American spirit during wartime by singing patriotic songs as part of our weekly assemblies in the school auditorium.

On these Wednesdays, our teacher led us in song using a pitch pipe, and sometimes we sang in rounds. We followed a special lyric sheet entitled, *Songs for the Home Front*.

It included favorites such as *Battle Hymn of the Republic*, as well as lesser-known compositions like *This Is Worth Fighting For*. The bottom of the sheet read, "Back the Attack with War Bonds and Stamps."

Shown as a 1950 high school senior in the photo at right, I still live in Amherst. And I'll never forget the patriotism my school displayed during the war.

—*Henrietta Cash, Amherst, Virginia*

BUNDLES OF JOY

It was in 1944, while I was in boot camp at the Great Lakes Naval Training Center in Illinois, that one of the fellows received a picture of his girlfriend in a bathing suit.

The neat photo of "Julie" eventually made the rounds in our barracks, and someone got the idea that maybe we should each write a letter to thank her for brightening our day.

Every member of Company 1748, even those who seldom wrote to anyone, composed an appreciative letter, and all of the letters went out in one mailing. Julie was about to be flooded with mail from 99 sailors.

Instead of getting mess hall duty during the week, I lucked out and was assigned to the post office. One day, when the mailbags came in, we received several bundles of letters, all from the same address. They were Julie's replies.

It turned out that Julie had recruited her girlfriends to help her respond. Together, they personally answered each and every one of our letters with a nice letter from "home."

—*Joseph Drobny, Marquette, Michigan*

in the NAVY

A FATHER AND THREE SONS ANSWERED THEIR COUNTRY'S WARTIME CALL.

FOUR FOR AMERICA. "My father-in-law, Albert Freitag Jr., served in the Navy during World War I, and three of his sons followed suit in World War II. This photograph was snapped at my father-in-law's house in Brookfield, Illinois," relates Louise Freitag, who lives in Oak Park. Shown with Albert Freitag Jr. (second from left) are his sons (from left) Earl, Albert III and Dick.

WASHED WHITES. "One of the sons must have been home on leave and needed his uniform cleaned," relates Louise Freitag. "It was left to dry on the family clothesline."

PROUD VETERAN. During the 1930s, Albert Freitag Jr. (front row, center) served as commander of the Edward Feely American Legion Post in Brookfield and marched in parades down Grand Boulevard.

raising the flag

While on a camping trip in the Colorado Mountains in 1965, these girlfriends didn't forget to commemorate the Fourth of July. "I took a picture of my friend Rena saluting while Marilyn raised a mini flag on our car antenna," says Jane Jackson Coates of Mill Creek, Washington. "We then proudly recited the Pledge of Allegiance."

CHAPTER 2

From Sea to SHINING SEA

page 31

page 42

page 34

Mount Rushmore…the Grand Canyon…Niagara Falls…whether natural or manmade, America's landmarks and landscapes are without equal.

"I was about 5 years old the first time my parents took me to the Great Salt Lake in the early 1930s," remembers Dean Thornton of Salt Lake City, Utah.

"On the east side of the lake was a long white sandy beach. I recall my mother sitting on a blanket in the sand while my father took me into the water. He'd put me on my back and slowly lower his hands. Sure enough, I'd float like a cork in the salty water.

"People came in droves to picnic and cool off at the lake. On weekends, the beach got so crowded that sometimes there were cars from one resort to another, three or four rows deep.

"Today, there are many tourist attractions in Utah to compete with the Great Salt Lake. The sunsets over the turquoise lake haven't changed, though. They're still just as spectacular as when it was the biggest recreation area in all of Utah."

Let this chapter take you on a trip around the U.S. and marvel at the beauty of our country.

page 37

Carving Mount Rushmore

FAMILY BROUGHT DAD LUNCH ATOP MOUNT RUSHMORE AS HE SHAPED THE PRESIDENTS.

By Maxine Evans, Manteca, California

In 1935, my father became a carver of granite presidents in the Black Hills of South Dakota.

The Bell Telephone Co. in Rapid City had just laid off my dad, George Rumple, when a miner friend asked him if he'd be interested in working on the Mount Rushmore monument. It was the Great Depression, and my father, who had a wife and three kids to support, jumped at the chance.

Gutzon Borglum, the great man of the mountain and the chief sculptor, asked my dad if he had any experience with such a project. He was hired to do some work on the road leading up to the mountain and did well. Borglum promoted him to work on the grand project.

Dad's records show that he made anywhere from 50 cents an hour as a laborer, in 1936, to $1.25 an hour as a foreman and then a carver, from 1936 to 1941.

When I was just 4 years old, in 1936, I heard my parents talk about the more than 750 stairs the workers had to climb. I recall going with my mother, Gladys, to take lunch to my dad on the top of Mount Rushmore. We'd sometimes walk up the many steps or ride up in a hoist "bucket."

FRUITS OF THEIR LABOR. The author is shown at right with her parents in 1941. Above: Mount Rushmore as it looks today.

I also met the two Native Americans who smoked a peace pipe at the top of the mountain to ensure no harm would come to the almost 400 workers involved with the project. They let me try the peace pipe, although I didn't actually smoke it! No one died during the 14-year project, which ran from 1927 to 1941.

My father told me he worked on the eyes of Thomas Jefferson and on the facial features of Abraham Lincoln. He even gave George Washington a haircut.

After dynamiting strategic spots, the workers used drills and jackhammers to create holes in the granite for easier carving. I remember hearing the explosions and seeing the white clouds of dust from the blasts.

I also recall President Franklin D. Roosevelt coming to see the mountain in 1936 for the dedication of the Thomas Jefferson head.

Nearby Keystone is where my brothers, Glen and Lyle, and I attended school. When work ended on the project in 1941, we moved to the state of Washington and then to California.

Standing on the top of Mount Rushmore is still an awesome memory for me, and Dad always referred to the Mount Rushmore memorial as the "No. 1 wonder of the world."

A PEACE PIPE used by Chief Black Horse (left) and Ben Black Elk, who posed with the author's father, was intended to ensure the workers' safety.

Monuments to America

WALKING IN D.C. "On Easter Sunday in 1954, my wife was all dolled up while posing near the Jefferson Memorial in Washington, D.C.," writes Clifton Harkey from Columbia, South Carolina. At the time, Clifton was in the Air Force.

AT THE WHITE HOUSE. The Burkett family of Magnolia, Ohio visited the president's residence in 1952. From left are Hicks, Nancy, Dick (age 1-1/2), Bea and David.

It is not what we have that will make us a great nation; it is the way in which we use it.

—Theodore Roosevelt

AH, SUMMER! Marty Kocman (above) cruised in a rowboat in 1956. In another vacation photo from 1961, he displayed his catch with brother Jan and the author.

In the Northwoods

By Frances Sabo, Springfield, Illinois

Waiting for the last two weeks of August to arrive was almost too much to bear for three children growing up in northwest Indiana during the 1950s.

When the much-anticipated time finally came, our favorite uncle, Eddie, would arrive at our house. Then we'd load up the car and head out for a summer vacation among the beautiful forests and lakes of Eagle River, Wisconsin.

During the trip, our excitement only grew. My two older brothers were the lucky ones—they got to sit in the back seat next to Uncle Eddie. Being the youngest, I had to sit in the front seat between Mom and Dad.

Our dog, Patches, lay at Mom's feet near our picnic lunch. We were packed in like sardines, but we loved every minute of it.

Cars didn't have air-conditioning in those days, and August in the Midwest was sweltering. There was no bypass around Milwaukee back then, so we had to drive through the city and wait at endless stoplights in the heat.

Finally we arrived in Eagle River. After loading up on food at the local grocery store, we headed for our rental cabin at Halicki's Housekeeping Cottages.

Thinking back on these trips, it sure wasn't much of a vacation for Mom. With the cabin's lack of modern conveniences, she did more work there than she did at home! But she smiled through all of it.

We spent much of our time swimming, hunting for frogs, cruising in the rowboat and just playing the day away, whether in the water or on shore.

Fishing was also a favorite pastime for me and my brothers, Marty and Jan. We caught some pretty respectable fish in the lake.

All too soon, our fun-filled summer vacation was over—and we were already looking forward to the next time we'd be heading up north.

MONUMENTAL STOP. Members of the Addington family posed near the Statue of Liberty during a trip around the U.S. From left are Mark, Betsy, John, Paul and their dad, Jack.

sticking to a travel budget

By Jack Addington, Rowlett, Texas

In 1966, our family of six set off on a trip to see 19 states and Canada in 21 days—with a budget of only $600.

The trip came in under budget, and we saw all the sights we planned to see, as our collection of souvenir window stickers shows. I have fond memories of that trip as I look at the many stickers we collected. They are a visible and nostalgic reminder of the states and historic sights my wife, Ann, and our four children visited together.

We left our home in Dallas, Texas, in our 1964 Ford Falcon station wagon. To economize, we slept on cots at national and state parks, or sometimes just on the side of the road. Many of our meals were cooked over a wood fire. And everywhere we went, we looked for window stickers to commemorate our visit.

We saw Niagara Falls and Monticello. Camping near the Great Lakes and in the Adirondack Mountains was breathtaking.

We also toured Washington, D.C., Philadelphia and New York City. It was in New York that we got some extra help staying within our budget.

An uncle who lived in a fancy Manhattan apartment let us camp out on the floor. I can still remember the curiosity of passers-by as the doorman let us double-park our dusty station wagon with its ugly roof rack while we unloaded pillows and blankets.

Another thing I remember about New York City is that we couldn't find any state window stickers.

Each of our children, then ages 6, 8, 9 and 11, had a duty, such as reading the map, building a campfire or keeping

34

tabs on expenses. We had it planned that if we stuck to our budget, we could splurge and go to a motel every fourth day. We managed to do it.

The trip taught me never to be surprised at anything. At Niagara Falls, for example, I was the last one to get out of the car and walk over to a low wall where we could view the falls.

There I found Ann and the kids, looking not at the majestic falls but at a mother spider and her babies busy with daily chores.

I guess the spider was as much of a natural wonder as the falls. But I did coax the kids to stand up and see Niagara, and they were thrilled again when we took the tour that led us below and behind the falls.

Every sticker we found went onto a window in the station wagon. Unfortunately, we were not able to find a sticker for every place we visited.

With only 30 more miles to go before reaching home, we stopped at a Stuckey's. And what did we find? Stickers from every state in the union.

We still laugh about that.

Ann has passed away, but the children and I still talk about the trip and the memories those great window stickers bring back.

STICKER STICKLERS. After 21 days on the road, Jack and Ann Addington and their four children were back home, showing off many stickers on their car.

Mountains to Climb

A ROCKY VACATION

I was 18 years old and feeling adventurous. It was 1952, and I'd just graduated from high school. My 11-year-old brother and I decided it was time to take a vacation like city folks took.

The two-week trip to Colorado would be our first vacation ever. We tried to figure out what our total expenses would be if everything went as planned.

We'd sleep in my 1931 Model A Ford and camp along our route. The car got about 25 miles per gallon, so we estimated about $40 of expenses ahead.

My brother was the map expert as we left Kansas and got on our way. We stopped at Castle Rock in western Kansas before reaching Denver, where we visited the zoo. Then we camped in a park in Colorado Springs.

Dinner that night was interesting. We made soup with water from the park's mineral springs, and it fizzed out of the pan! It turned out the water was naturally carbonated. We mixed it with orange juice to make soda pop.

On another night, we camped on a ridge above an Old West town named Black Hawk. We could hear ragtime tunes coming from a piano in a saloon below and felt like we were in a Western movie.

We didn't know that the cost of gas would be much higher in the mountains than in the plains. Diesel was the cheaper option, and at one point we tried filling the car with a mix.

The result was a trail of smoke behind the car! Finally, a highway patrolman stopped us and asked, "Are you trying to make the Smokies out of the Rockies?" He was very nice and wished us well on our vacation, but he advised us to go back to using only gasoline, no matter how pricey it was.

At Garden of the Gods Park, I set about using my skills as a budding artist. Getting out my oil paints, I tried my hand at capturing the beauty of the reddish rocks.

My brother had fun looking for small rocks to take home. But his collection kept getting bigger, and I eventually had to put a stop to it. Our little Model A was having a tough time climbing the Rocky Mountains as it was, without a load of rocks!

All too soon, it was time to head back east. After visiting Boot Hill back in Kansas, we had a flat tire in Dodge City, and I had to purchase a used tire at a filling station for $15. Luckily, it was the only problem we had with the car during the entire trip.

It was a great two weeks of freedom, fun and adventure for me and my little brother to share and remember.

And with all the jars of carbonated mineral water we brought back with us, we were making our own soda pop for quite some time.

—By Jim Brownrigg, Iola, Kansas

> I don't know what you could say about a day in which you have seen four beautiful sunsets.
>
> —John Glenn

PEEK FROM THE PEAK. "This is my husband, Marion, and me with our two children, Doug and Kathleen, at the top of Engineer Mountain, near Silverton, Colorado," says Ardie Bell Cunningham, who lives northwest of the peak in Grand Junction. "The photo was taken in 1957. We were sitting at an altitude of 12,980 feet."

HIGH CHAIR. "In this photo, my wife, Marla, and her father, Joe Braaksma, are riding up Wyoming's Snow King Mountain on a chair lift," says Ev Cope of Bozeman, Montana. "They were on a trip from their home in Churchill, Montana in 1955. In the background are the Tetons and the city of Jackson Hole. Marla's older brother, Joe Jr., was in a chair by himself behind them, and her mother, Martha, was in another chair. It was quite an event for them to pay for a photo."

Riding The
SNOW KING MT'N
CHAIR LIFT
Jackson. Wyo.
16 AUG 1955

Golden Getaways

CALIFORNIA CAMPING

Luxuries were few for most people during the years of the Great Depression, and our family was no exception.

We were fortunate that Dad had found a good job in the oil fields near Goleta, California, shortly before the Depression hit, and that he held the job throughout those hard times. He even got two weeks of vacation each year.

My mother, sister and I really looked forward to those times off. It was our summer vacation, an escape from the daily grind of the Depression.

An outdoorsman who loved to hunt and fish, Dad always took us camping. We'd go to a California park or to one of the state's many lakes, including Huntington, Clear, June and Blue lakes.

When I was 6 years old, Dad made a trailer to pull behind our 1936 Nash Rambler (above). In the trailer were tents, cots, blankets, canned food, a Coleman stove, a lantern and fuel.

Dad also made a cooler for butter and meat out of wire and plywood. He'd soak burlap in water and drape it down the wire sides. We made sure to hang the cooler in a tree, high enough so the bears couldn't get it at night.

At Big Basin Redwoods State Park, we had to watch out for the deer, too. They looked tame, but they could be aggressive, coming right up to your table for food.

Some of my favorite trips were to Yosemite National Park (shown above in 1939). It had an amphitheater with log benches, where the nightly entertainment included park staff dumping garbage onstage to attract bears. Visitors could sit and watch the bears come and eat.

At the close of the evening, we watched the park's "firefall." Staffers created the illusion of a waterfall of fire by pushing burning coals over a sheer cliff. What a sight for little kids to see!

We also had fun among Yosemite's giant sequoias. One of the big trees was carved out so cars could drive right through it.

I have many fond memories of our summer trips during this bygone era. Life was hard, but we found a way to have wonderful times together.

—*Erwin Langlo, Santa Maria, California*

SEEING THE SIGHTS

In the summer of 1952, our dad, Henry DuBois, took my brothers, Don and Ed, my sister, Kathy, and me on a month-long trip from Waukegan, Illinois, to California and back.

These pictures (left and below left) are some of the photos Dad took along the way using a Stereo Realist 3-D camera as we saw Mount Rushmore, Yellowstone, the Grand Canyon, Yosemite and so on. In the picture with the bear, Don is standing by our 1951 Kaiser and Ed is leaning out the window.

When we passed through Death Valley, California, after midnight, the temperature was still 125 degrees after a near-record high of 132 that day. In the top photo, you can see the swamp cooler attached to the side of the car. We used a windshield washer squeeze bulb to spray water on the radiator as we drove up the hills.

—*Chet DuBois, Zion, Illinois*

BIG TREE MEMORIES

The highlight of our trip to Yosemite National Park in 1935, when I was 7 years old, was the drive through the giant sequoia known as the Wawona Tunnel Tree.

My father, Roy, took a photo of my mother, Alma, and me in our Plymouth with his Brownie box camera.

In 1951, while we on our honeymoon, my wife, Jane, and I had a picture taken in our Dodge (right) as we posed by the same tree for a souvenir snapshot taken by a park photographer.

The tunnel was cut through the tree in 1881, when it was estimated to be 2,500 years old. The tree finally fell in 1969 during a winter of heavy snow, and the road was closed all winter.

—*Roy Nichols Jr., Reno, Nevada*

Grand Adventure

AN OLD MAN FASCINATED TWO LITTLE GIRLS WITH HIS STORIES. YEARS LATER, THEY LEARNED HE WAS A PIECE OF AMERICA'S PAST.

By June Emslie, San Bernardino, California

Back in 1925, our parents took my sister, Bertha May, and me on a trip to the Grand Canyon. I was only 4 years old at the time, but so many details of that memorable trip still stand out clearly in my mind today—especially a colorful character who befriended us.

My parents had pitched a tent to serve as our sleeping quarters near the canyon. One night, an old gentleman with red hair and a long beard stopped by our campsite and asked if he could share our fire.

When my parents said yes, he offered to tell my sister and me some stories he recalled from the Old West…and I'll never forget the exciting tales he told.

Wide-eyed, we listened with rapt attention to stories about his meetings with Wild Bill Hickok, Calamity Jane and Buffalo Bill.

He was such good company that my parents invited him back to share our campfire several other evenings!

A Picture for Proof

On the last day of our vacation, before Bertha May and I were sent off to bed for the night, the old gentleman told us about his two donkeys, Temporary and Dynamite. Temporary was nice and gentle, but Dynamite was mean and ornery.

The old cowpoke promised my sister and me that before we left for home the next morning, he'd put us on Temporary's back so my folks could take a picture of us.

He was true to his word. Standing proudly

next to Temporary in the photograph my dad took was R. Earle Gardener. On the back of the photo, my mother made a note that Mr. Gardener was 78 years old.

Years passed. In 1937, we were living in Arkansas City, Kansas. By then, Bertha May and I were in high school.

One Sunday morning, Mother looked up from the newspaper and exclaimed, "Wait until you hear this!"

Story of an Old Friend

She read aloud an article that described a pioneer couple who'd gone west in a covered wagon with their baby son sometime during the last century.

The wagon was attacked by Indians and the couple killed, but when the Indians discovered the child, they were intrigued by his red hair and decided to spare him.

He was raised as an Indian, and eventually spotted by some cavalry soldiers when he was nearly grown. The soldiers convinced him that he was not really an Indian. From that time on, he served as a scout for the army.

Mother said, "This is the story of R. Earle Gardener, the very same man who sat with us and told us those stories around the campfire at the Grand Canyon!"

According to the story, Mr. Gardener— then nearly 90—had written a complete account of his life but wouldn't let anyone publish it until after his death.

Unfortunately, it never was published as far as I know, although *Life* magazine did publish a picture of "old soldier R.E. Gardener" in a 1972 story on the 100th anniversary of Yellowstone National Park.

Now, of course, I'm sorry I never saved that article. Still, I'll always cherish my "brush with the Wild West" and memories of an old Indian scout who made a trip to the Grand Canyon even more exciting for two little girls.

GOLLY, WHAT A GULLEY!
In this photo from 1949, Tom Pearson (foreground) had just led riders on mules into the Grand Canyon. "I worked as a tour guide there for eight years, and I never got tired of the beautiful scenery," he writes from Dolan Springs, Arizona.

winter wonderland

NARROW PATH. Heavy snow left room for only one car at a time on this country bridge (right) near Doylestown, Pennsylvania. Ruth and Earl Hunsberger of Davidsville shared the photograph; they were managing a nearby farm at the time.

POLAR EXPLORERS. "My wife, Dot, and son Don were on a winter outing in the area around Oak Ridge, Tennessee, when these slides (above and left) were taken in 1947," says Gene Pierce of Kingston. "I worked at the Oak Ridge National Laboratory from 1944 to 1980, and Don got a job there as an engineer."

On the Jersey Shore

LEISURELY WALK. "My husband, George, and his family are seen in 1930 on their annual stroll at Atlantic City's boardwalk," says Elaine Langford of Millsboro, Delaware. "From left are Albert Jr., Albert, George, Elsie and the kids' maternal grandparents, Carrie and Harold Widmark."

LEONARDO BEACH. "In the early 1900s, my grandparents, great-uncles and great-aunt built two bungalows side by side in New Monmouth, New Jersey," says Linda Spiak of Margate, Florida. "Our family spent every summer weekend on Leonardo Beach. The photo at far right shows my mom, Elizabeth Jelly, and her mother, Florence, in 1946. The earlier photo shows Grandma on the left with my mom and great-aunt Myrtle Parson."

A QUAINT COTTAGE held years of summer memories. The children were responsible for raising the flag (below).

island summer

TRIPS TO THE LONG ISLAND SHORE WERE GLORIOUS FOR SUBURBAN KIDS.

By Judy Moore, San Pedro, California

At the end of the school year, my family would flee the New York City suburbs and drive at the breakneck speed of 25 to 30 mph out to the eastern shores of Long Island.

On the inside shore of the northern peninsula was our little piece of heaven, a cottage near Jamesport. The rented cottage sat alone in a field of tall grass about 100 yards from Flanders Bay. Farther down the road, almost out of sight, was a year-round house. Other than that, we were quite alone.

The rustic cottage included two bedrooms, an all-purpose living room and a primitive kitchen. Electric service consisted of single light bulbs hanging in the middle of each room.

The plumbing was a simple hand pump in the kitchen; our only other "plumbing" was a two-seater outhouse across the dirt road, near some bushes and poison ivy.

The cottage is where I spent some of the first summers of my life, from 1936 to 1945.

We children were free to roam and explore. We swam, climbed trees, rowed our boat, rode our bikes, dug out hiding places in the bushes, played croquet and caught butterflies and fiddler crabs—but only after our chores were done.

My mother's day was quite different. She spent much of her time in the crude kitchen with an icebox, a three-burner kerosene stove, a two-burner hot plate and a portable oven that was moved from burner to burner.

Mother did the laundry by hand with a washboard, pumping the water and then heating it on the stove. What a job—oh, the aching knuckles! She took it all in stride, although she did say that she had to get a vitamin shot after we returned to civilization.

During the workweek, Daddy stayed in the suburbs with my grandmother, but on summer weekends, he was ours. He rode the Cannonball Express to Jamesport every Friday evening. My middle sister, Carol, and I would compete to see who would be the first to see his train as it came down the railroad tracks, belching great plumes of smoke.

Then, there was Daddy, stepping down from the railway platform, the pockets of his business suit filled with Chiclets or Life Savers candy for us.

A good part of the weekend was spent fishing. Daddy loved to fish and taught us how to bait a hook and set it when we felt a nibble on the line. We learned how to clean the fish and prepare them for a meal.

As much as I loved being with my father, I would dissolve into tears when I saw the poor fish dangling from the barbed hook. I would beg Daddy to return it to the water, which he always did. Pretty soon, I was no longer invited to go on these family expeditions.

When we saw the swallows, we knew it was time to leave behind the lovely warm sunny days of our summer vacation.

Before returning to the suburbs, however, we underwent the olive-oil ritual. The salt water of the bay and the baking sun had turned our hair into wild, wiry "frizz bombs."

My mom's remedy was to drench our heads

TRANSPORTATION for the author, in 1942, was a two-wheeler. "Those summer days passed much too quickly," she says.

with olive oil, which had to stay on all day—no swimming underwater during the day. In the evening, we would undergo several shampoos and thus be made presentable for suburban society.

I still relive these summers in my mind. Our cottage getaways were a wonderful gift from my parents that has carried me through the many difficult times that we all have to face in life. For this, I am eternally grateful.

A TRIP FOR TWO. On a visit to Niagara Falls, New York, in September of 1959, newlyweds Rudy and Joan Dziedzic took time out for a quick snapshot. "We lived in the Williamsburg area of Brooklyn, and the ride was always very nice," says Joan, whose birth name was Schipani. "It's so beautiful there. I now live in my parents' Brooklyn home, which we children inherited from them."

TOP O' THE WORLD.

"My mother and father, Florence and Willis Townsend, went to the top of the Empire State Building on their honeymoon in 1935," says Angela Townsend of Miami Beach, Florida. "Dad was a 77-year-old widower and Mom was only 27. He was in great health and they had four children in nine years. Dad lived to be 90."

EMPIRE STATE BUILDING
NEW YORK

TALLEST STRUCTURE IN THE WORLD
1248 FEET HIGH   102 STORIES

...s and Appetizers

...20c Fresh Fruit	35c
...ouillon	15c
	20c
	20c
...ice Cocktail	20c

...Salads

...Potato & Sardine	65c
Crabflake Salad	
with Egg & Tomato	
& Russian Dressing	80c
Potato, Tomato &	
Egg	80c
Chicken Salad	85c
Asparagus & Egg	75c
Sliced Ham & Potato	
Salad with Tomato	80c
Tomato Stuffed with	
Chicken	90c
...Assorted Cold Cuts	80c
...With Chicken	95c
...Tomato with Shrimp	80c
...d with Salads	5c

...ches

...Chicken Salad	70c
...lam & Tomato	60c
...ombination	65c
...Sliced Chicken	70c
...Liverwurst	40c
Smithfield-Ham	
& Chopped Egg	60c
...Sardine	50c
Cream Cheese on	
Date & Nut Bread	40c
Chicken, Ham, &	
Tomato	90c

Tuna Fish	50c
Baked Ham	55c
Sliced Egg	40c
Salmon	50c
Shrimp Salad	50c
Tomato & Lettuce	40c
Cream Cheese &	
Olive	35c
Cream Cheese &	
Nut	40c

Special 25c
Cinnamon Toast
(on Whole Wheat Raisin Bread)
Tea · Coffee · Milk

Special 70c
Any 35c or 45c Sandwich
Small Ice Cream
Tea · Coffee · Milk

Special 80c
Waldorf Salad
Cinnamon Toast
Cup Cake
Tea · Coffee · Milk

Special 80c
Stuffed Egg
Combination Salad
Mayonnaise Dressing
Roll and Butter
Ice Cream
Tea · Coffee · Milk
· Roll or Bread with Butter 5c

Special 35c
Toasted English Muffin
Jam or Marmalade
Tea · Coffee · Milk

Special 80c
Salmon or Tuna Fish
& Vegetable Salad
Special Cake or Ice Cream
Tea · Coffee · Milk

Special 80c
Assorted Sandwiches
Ice Cream
Tea · Coffee · Milk

Special 85c
Fresh Fruit Salad
with Celery
Buttered Nut Bread
Tea · Coffee · Milk

Special 95c
Fruit Salad and Assorted
Canapes
Ice Cream or Special Cake
Tea · Coffee · Milk

No Change or Substitutions on Specials
Iced Tea - Iced Coffee on 75c and 85c Specials Only
Iced Tea · Iced Coffee on all others · 5c extra
Only One Cup of Coffee per Customer

WINES AND LIQUORS
SEE WINE LIST

Desserts

Apple Pie	20c	Cheese & Crackers	25c
Special Layer Cake	15c	Date and Nut Bread	
		with Butter	15c
Special Pie	20c	Saltines	10c
Pie a la mode	30c	Social Tea	10c

Beverages

Coffee - Cup 10c	Iced - 20c	Per Pot	25c
Orange Pekoe Tea-Cup 10c	Iced-20c	Per Pot	25c
Hot Chocolate	15c	Iced	20c
Milk - (Bottle)			10c
Coca Cola	10c	Lemon and Lime sm.	10c
Large Coca Cola	15c	Lemon and Lime lg.	15c
Root Beer	10c	Large Root Beer	15c

Fresh Fruit Drinks
(in Season)

Grape Fruit Juice	20c	Lemonade	25c
Grape Juice	20c	Limeade	25c
Lime Rickey	25c	Orangeade	25c
Grape Juice Lime-			
ade	25c	Grape Fruit Juice	
Orange Juice	25c	Limeade	25c

Fountain Drinks

Milk Shake—Any Flavor		20c
Ice Cream Sodas—Any Flavor		20c
Sundaes		25c
Large Plate Ice Cream 25c—Small		15c
Malted Milk—All Flavors	25c—With Egg	30c
Frosted Drinks—All Flavors	25c—With Egg	30c
Milk Floats—All Flavors	25c—With Egg	30c

BIG SPLURGE IN BIG APPLE.

"In 1944, while I was in training for the Coast Guard in New York, my girlfriend, later my wife, came to visit," recalls Robert Gurn of Franklin, Wisconsin. "We had dinner at the restaurant in the Empire State Building. I took this menu as a souvenir and have kept it all these years. It's interesting to look at the prices and compare them to what restaurants charge today."

CALL IT WHAT YOU WILL — a fortunate conjunction of the planets, or the inscrutable march of events, *or just plain good luck*—but 1939 has brought to America the most amazing cycle of fun, excitement and thrills in its fast-moving history!

Shining stars in this galaxy are the New York World's Fair and the Golden Gate Exposition—world events no American should miss. Sprinkled between, on this giant coast-to-coast orbit, are the scarcely lesser lights of vacation enchantment—cool and wondrous national parks, northern lakes and mountains, surf-swept beaches, dude ranches—fishing, hunting, riding—every summer scene and sport in the catalogue.

"I can't see them all in my short vacation, on my small budget," say you. But you can! That's where Greyhound

steps into the picture, with the amazing rate of $69.95 to both Fairs and a hundred places of thrilling interest in between—over any route you may wish to travel, from your home, across the continent to New York, to San Francisco, and back home again.

"But I simply can't take time to see both Fairs," you come back (wistfully). Well then—visit whichever Fair you've set your heart upon, throw in a cool vacation resort or two, pack the trip into as few or as many days as you wish—and still save dollars over any other type of transportation that rolls, swims, or flies.

A great fleet of Greyhound Super-Coaches, streamlined, smooth-rolling—efficiently ventilated or completely air-conditioned—awaits your pleasure when you gaily "swing around America this summer."

GRANDEST CIRCLE TOUR IN TRAVEL HISTORY— *visiting both Fairs...*

for only

$69.95

This amazingly low rate includes transportation from your home, across the continent to one Fair, then back to the other, and return to your home—following your choice of scenic routes. You can take as much as ninety days— or the trip can easily be made in two weeks. It's an all-time bargain, no matter how you plan it.

Ask about Expense-Paid Tours . . . they save time and money, add pleasure, assure hotel reservations.

Principal Greyhound Information Offices

The **GREYHOUND** LINES

CLEVELAND, O. . . . . . East 9th & Superior
PHILADELPHIA, PA. . . Broad Street Station
NEW YORK CITY . . . . . 245 West 50th St.
CHICAGO, ILL. . . . . . 12th & Wabash
BOSTON, MASS. . . . . . 60 Park Square
WASHINGTON, D. C. . . . . 1403 New York Ave., N. W.
DETROIT, MICH. . . . . . Washington Blvd. at Grand River
ST. LOUIS, MO. . . Broadway & Delmar Blvd.
CHARLESTON, W. VA. . . . 155 Summers St.

SAN FRANCISCO, CAL. . . Pine & Battery Sts.
FT. WORTH, TEX. . . . . . 905 Commerce St.
MINNEAPOLIS, MINN. . . 509 Sixth Ave., N.
MEMPHIS, TENN. . . . . . 527 N. Main St.
NEW ORLEANS, LA. . . . 400 N. Rampart St.
LEXINGTON, KY. . . . . . 801 N. Limestone
CINCINNATI, O. . . . . . 630 Walnut St.
RICHMOND, VA. . . . . . 412 E. Broad St.
WINDSOR, ONT. . . . 403 Ouellette Ave.
LONDON, ENGLAND . . . . A. B. Reynoldson, 49 Leadenhall Street

This Brings Pictorial World's Fair Booklets, Full Information

Mail this coupon to nearest Greyhound information office, listed at left, for bright, informational, pictorial folders all about the NEW YORK WORLD'S FAIR ☐, or SAN FRANCISCO'S GOLDEN GATE EXPOSITION ☐. Please check the one desired. No cost or obligation to you. If you want special information on any other trip, jot down place you wish to visit, on line below.

Information on trip to_____

Name_____

Address_____ SP-6

Beach
BLISS

HOW HOT WAS IT? "It was so hot, the children were standing on a rag to keep their feet from burning on the asphalt," remembers Loretta Clark of Albion, New York. "I took this picture of my nieces and neighbors in Boynton Beach, Florida, in the summer of 1960 with a little box camera I'd received for selling salve."

BALANCING ACT. "Here I am with Walter, about a month after we got engaged, in 1955. We spent a wonderful day with friends at the lighthouse in Montauk, New York," says Angela Smith of Wantagh.

If you come to a fork in the road, take it.

—Yogi Berra

long way from home

"My cousins Ron (at left) and Bob Burghauser were sporting their Baltimore Orioles shirts while camping in Yellowstone National Park," writes Carol Burghauser, who lives in Baltimore, Maryland. "The trip was in July 1966. My late uncle Rudy Burghauser of Dundalk took the picture."

CHAPTER 3

We Can
DO IT

page 66

page 58

page 65

That never-give-up attitude—it's a part of our nation's character. No matter how difficult the challenge or how daunting the task, Americans face it with a don't-quit, keep-on-trying mentality.

"I had great role models when it came to overcoming adversity. They were my grandparents," says Susanna Lahde of Nashville, Tennessee.

"Mammaw and Daddad experienced many hardships in their lives. Daddad almost died when he contracted tetanus after a farm accident. In 1925, their home was destroyed by a tornado.

"They started over and bought a hardware store, only to see it ravaged by fire several years later. The snack shop they opened next was almost robbed—Mammaw talked the would-be robber out of it.

"She cared for Daddad when he suffered dementia, and she fought to walk again after breaking her hip. They always stayed strong, looked trouble square in the eye and found a way to go on."

With stories about the Great Depression, World War II and more, this chapter is a testament to those with that indomitable American spirit.

page 69

STARTING OUT.
The author's parents
are shown in their
wedding photo
in 1913.

Steps to Make Ends Meet

MOM AND DAD WENT THE EXTRA MILE—AND FOOT—TO PROVIDE FOR A FAMILY OF 10 DURING THE DEPRESSION.

By Charles Taylor Jr., St. Simons Island, Georgia

Raising eight children in a house with two bedrooms, a small kitchen and one bathroom is no easy task. But that's just what my parents did during the hardships of the 1930s.

Charles Spurgeon Taylor and Ollie Hubbard were married in 1913 and moved into a home in Danville, Virginia, the same year. By the time the stock market crashed and the Depression struck in 1929, they had six children. Two more would be born by 1933.

My father worked 5½ days per week in a knitting mill while my mother stayed home to take care of the children. After the economic downturn, Dad was put on a short workweek.

Like many people in those difficult days, we faced struggle and sacrifice. But we always managed to have food on the table, thanks to my parents' thrifty ways.

Having grown up on farms, Mom and Dad knew how to grow and preserve food. They put that knowledge to good use during the Depression. I don't know what our grocery bill was, but it must have been pretty low.

In the backyard, we had peach, cherry and apple trees and a vegetable garden along the

banks of a small creek. Granddaddy Hubbard, who lived down the road from us, would bring his mule and plow to get the ground ready for seed each spring.

Hatching Plans

Our backyard was big enough to accommodate two large poultry houses, too. Somehow, Dad found time to build them.

To get their chicken production going, my parents invested in a poultry brooder. This enclosed contraption was equipped with lightbulbs that generated enough heat to hatch a large number of eggs placed just beneath them.

I can't recall how long it took for the eggs to hatch, but we kids were there to watch the little chicks break out of their shells. The brooder was kept in our bedroom!

Mom canned much of our homegrown harvest for the winter months. With our little orchard, the vegetable garden, the chickens and eggs, we never went hungry.

To save even more money, Dad took another economical step. He acquired a shoe last that he used to repair our footwear.

The shoe last was an iron foot-shaped form in a heavy wood-block base. Using this tool, Dad could hammer new leather or rubber soles and heels onto our old shoes, making them wearable again. To us kids, all of these thrifty measures were very important for one reason. They meant we could get 5 cents a week as a candy allowance!

I still have that old shoe last. It occupies a place of honor in our breakfast room, and my wife and I pass by it many times each day.

Battered and well used, the shoe last is a reminder to me of bygone years when people faced life's hard knocks on their own—and came through all the better for it.

Through the Depression

ALL THAT FUN FOR A DIME

My father (at right) was always full of fun, even during the Great Depression when our lives were the hardest. One way or another, he kept life interesting for us five kids when we were growing up in Waterloo, Iowa.

I remember several times, when he had hardly two coins to jingle together in his much-patched pockets, he announced out of the blue that he had hidden a dime somewhere in our house.

It would be in plain sight, he said—nothing had to be lifted, opened or looked under. We could find the dime with both hands clasped behind our backs.

The hunt was on! Sometimes it took an hour or two of enthusiastic searching to find the dime, as visions of licorice, suckers and jawbreakers danced through our heads.

For the life of me, I can't remember who the lucky ones were who discovered those dimes. But I do recall with great fondness the simple games my father dreamed up to entertain us and brighten our days.

—*Phoebe Borden Witzel, Oceanside, California*

FAMOUS FLOAT

Making a living was especially difficult during the Depression. My father, Paul Ruecker, built this root beer stand in the early 1930s to supplement his income as a plumbing contractor in Minneapolis-St. Paul.

Two of my sisters, Frieda and Margaret, and my brother Herb are in the photo. It was taken after Prohibition had been repealed, as shown by the beer signs.

One day, Herb made a drink for his girlfriend, who did the books, and put ice cream in her soda. A few days later, he did the same thing with root beer. To this day, we're convinced Herb invented the root beer float.

—Ray Ruecker, Mesa, Arizona

BURYING THE 'OLD MAN'

In 1933, many people in our small town were struggling with the economic hardships of the time. On Memorial Day, we found a way to "end" the Depression—symbolically, at least.

The holiday festivities that day in Lake Butler, Florida, included the dedication of a newly constructed bridge. As the dedication got under way, our local American Legion post led a group of beautiful girls across the bridge, followed by Boy Scouts, war veterans and public officials.

At last, spectators were invited to gather near the bridge in a little churchyard on the hill. They unpacked picnic baskets and spread their lunches as the band played *Happy Days Are Here Again,* a favorite tune of the time, and politicians gave speeches.

My young sister and I were allowed to roam through the crowd, and we came upon what

looked like a fresh grave near the church door. A crude sign read, "Old Man Depression." Only a small, wilted bouquet of yellow bitterweed flowers decorated the mound of earth. It was truly a pathetic sight.

Though we were young girls, we were old enough to know we ought to be respectful of the dead. So what we saw men do as they walked by shocked us.

They spat tobacco juice on the grave, kicked dirt on it and made disparaging remarks about the "old man." Not only that, they seemed to enjoy their antics, snapping their suspenders and laughing.

It was some years before I understood the reason for their behavior at the "grave." It was a way of saying, "These hard times won't get the best of us." I understood that I should be happy to say goodbye to Old Man Depression. And good riddance, too!

—Mary Sue Mosby, Canton, Mississippi

surviving the 'dirty thirties' took real grit

WHEN THE DARK DUST STORMS RAGED, LIFE CAME TO A STANDSTILL AND STREETLIGHTS TURNED ON IN THE DAYTIME.

By Dora Felix, Paramount, California

In the spring of 1935, we moved to the small town of Downs in north-central Kansas. My father, George DeBey, was a well-known real estate broker, and it wasn't long before property in Kansas and the surrounding states where Father did business was moving...literally.

We were living in the heart of the Dust Bowl, and that April, we experienced the true misery this term implied.

When we first moved into our big two-story house of concrete block, Mother washed the walls and windows until the place sparkled. I polished the cabinets, railings and doors. The frilly curtains Mother sewed created a friendly look, and the front porch, with its oversize swing, let us enjoy the fresh Kansas breezes.

Afterward, we relaxed and waited for spring rains to provide needed moisture. The breezes came, but they didn't bring rain—instead, they brought huge gray-black clouds of dust that robbed us of our peace and tranquility.

The breeze turned to howling winds as the bone-dry soil, loosely anchored to crops or other vegetation, was lifted up to blacken the sky. As far as we could see, the sky was dark.

Dust found its way into every crevice of the house. Mother and I soaked bedsheets in the bathtub, wrung them out and tacked them to the inside of the doors. Then we'd huddle around the radio (when it worked), trying to learn the extent of the storm.

When we finally ventured out on foot to get some groceries, we discovered that life in the town was at a standstill. Father's real estate business came to a complete halt.

It was so dark that the streetlights had been turned on. Our neighbor's chickens, confused

LIBERAL DUSTING. The '30s were dirty for the folks of Liberal, Kansas, in April 1935, when the dust storm shown in these photos from the author hit town. The howling winds brought dust that turned day into night, buried cars and filled houses with dirt.

about the day that had turned into night, gathered inside their coop to roost.

One time during the many days of swirling dust, we looked out and were surprised to see that every bit of the landscape had been tinted red. Oklahoma, not to be left out of the picture, had sent us some of its red soil from across the miles.

President Franklin Roosevelt's New Deal was no match for Mother Nature and couldn't stop the dust storms. But we were hopeful that it would eventually aid with any other problems we had.

With the indomitable spirit of our fellow Kansans, we survived the Dust Bowl, dusted ourselves off and looked toward a brighter future.

struggle with polio meant never giving up

THE FIGHT AGAINST THIS FEARED DISEASE TOOK YEARS, LOTS OF COURAGE AND PLENTY OF SUPPORT FROM LOVED ONES.

By Helen Perrine, Roseville, Illinois

I was just a country girl working in the big city of Chicago in 1949. While apartment hunting, I was not feeling up to par.

I thought I was getting the flu. It was an effort simply to step up on a curb. My legs just didn't want to function.

The next day I went to work as usual—I had a job as a secretary in sporting goods in Sears' mail-order department. But I soon ended up in the infirmary.

Although the doctors told me I was too ill to travel, I felt I just had to get home to my parents' farm in Berwick, Illinois. My sister Lois met me at the train and took me to a doctor in Monmouth. He said my temperature was normal and that I didn't have polio.

The next day, however, I couldn't even lift a hairbrush and had to have my legs lifted to get into the car and go back to the doctor.

Dreaded Diagnosis

This time, the doctor ordered a spinal tap. A positive report sent me to St. Mary's Hospital in Galesburg, where an X-ray room had been converted to an isolation ward for polio victims.

By the time I arrived, I could no longer move my legs and had only limited movement above the waist. A raging illness obliterated my mind for the next few days, and I was listed as gravely ill.

An iron lung was kept outside my hospital room, but a young nun I'll never forget, Sister Regina, stayed by my side and reminded me to breathe. The crisis passed.

For the next 8½ months, I underwent therapy at Methodist Hospital in Peoria. Oh, how good Sister Kenny's hot packs and whirlpool treatments felt on my stiff, sore body.

Later, I was fitted with braces, then went through more therapy to learn how to walk while wearing 16 pounds of steel and leather. I wore the braces for nine years, until 10 operations helped me get rid of them.

I married my fiance, Paul Perrine, a year after I got out of the hospital. He had stood by me during all those months of rehabilitation.

Paul and I went on to have 34 wonderful years together and three beautiful children.

BRAVE BATTLE. These photos from Helen Perrine show what life was like for polio victims in the 1940s and '50s. The "Hubbard Tank" (above) was used to soothe Helen's stiff and sore body. The braces she wore for nine years weighed 16 pounds (right). Helen's fiance, Paul (below right, in 1950), stuck by her through months of rehabilitation.

Never interrupt someone doing something you said couldn't be done.

—Amelia Earhart

CROSS-COUNTRY. The Hall family traveled to California in a homemade camper in 1946. The author is on the left in the family portrait taken a few years earlier (below), and under the window in the photo at far right.

Like a Scene From a Movie

By Calvin Hall, Ulysses, Kansas

Anyone who has seen *The Grapes of Wrath* has an idea what my family was like when we left home in search of a better life.

In the movie, members of a poor farm family pack up their belongings in an old, overloaded truck and leave Oklahoma for the promise of work in California.

We sure weren't much different. Our vehicle was a little better and we had some money. But like the characters in the film, we had a dream about living well in the "land of milk and honey."

In 1946, my father, Clarence Hall, heard from his sisters that jobs in the shipyards near San Diego were plentiful. Dad, who'd farmed during World War II, decided we should leave our home near Crawford, Oklahoma, and head west.

Mom and Dad had four young children at the time. I was about 5 years old, and the oldest of my three sisters was about 7.

Getting to California would be no easy feat. Dad was a good farm mechanic and blacksmith, and he had a 1934 Chevy that was in fairly good condition. He made up his mind to transform the car into a camper.

Dad had no electric drills or power tools. I remember him tearing into that car with a hacksaw and chisel. He did away with the doors, lengthened the frame and added a drag axle created from the front axle of an old Pontiac.

The camper had Masonite siding and a roof made from sheets of aluminum. It couldn't have been more than 24 feet long and 8 feet wide.

We packed our clothes in boxes and loaded them into the camper. When we left Oklahoma in the autumn of 1946, we headed for Amarillo, Texas, and turned onto Route 66.

On the Road

The camper had very few comforts or extras. We kids slept on cots on the floor and had no seats; we sat on either the floor or the bed that Mom and Dad shared.

Mom cooked in a "kitchen" consisting of a three-burner kerosene stove with an oven that she had to put over a burner. A little one-burner kerosene stove provided our heat.

On the way, we took just enough of a detour so that we could see the Grand Canyon. Mom wasn't enthused; she was scared of heights and was always afraid something bad would happen to us kids. She just knew one of us was going to tumble down into the canyon.

Disappointing Destination

After crossing from Arizona into California, we wound up in Madera. But by the time we arrived, the jobs Dad was qualified for were taken. He had to settle for gathering eggs at a chicken farm. Just as in the movie, California wasn't all it was cracked up to be!

We spent Christmas in Madera. Mom was expecting another baby and wanted to return to Oklahoma. Disappointed with the shortage of work in California, Dad didn't need much convincing. So, later that winter, our family left for home.

I vividly recall one day in particular during our return trip. In the mountainous area near Oatman, Arizona, our camper began to jump out of gear. We were on some of the steepest hairpin curves of Route 66.

Mom, who was seven months pregnant, had to sit in a makeshift seat with no back and hold the old transmission in gear. When she relaxed too much, it would jump out of low gear and Dad had to start all over again.

We finally decided to call it quits that day and made camp for the night so Dad could work on the transmission. It was unbearably cold on the side of the mountain, and a howling wind was shaking our camper.

We had just gotten into bed when we heard a strange banging noise outside. Mom got scared; she was convinced wild animals were going to claw their way inside the camper and devour my sisters and me.

Dad went outside to check things out—and came back in laughing his head off. He told us little mountain burros were clustered around the camper, trying to get a break from the wind and escape the cold.

We pushed on from there…and made it back to Oklahoma in time for my brother, Wayne, to be born on February 15, 1947.

The Long Hot Summer of 1948

HOEING WAS JUST THE BEGINNING OF THE WORK TO BE DONE DURING THAT UNFORGETTABLE SEASON.

By Myrtle Beavers, Destin, Florida

Having lived through the Great Depression and World War II as a young child, I had experienced a hardscrabble life before I was old enough to know it.

Our farm family faced many hardships during my childhood, but I'll always be proud of the ways we made it through together.

One particular summer stands out in my memory—the summer of 1948. I was barely 14 and had just finished the eighth grade.

During the previous year, there had been little rain and the crops on our farm in Hix, Oklahoma, were not doing well. My parents, Robert and Hattie Morton, were getting on in years, and with only the youngest two of 10 children still at home, they had to do much of the work themselves.

Unbeknownst to my little brother Dwayne and me, my parents had made a hard decision. Mama would find a job in town while Papa stayed on the farm.

Mama got a job as a dishwasher during the week. When the school year ended in 1948, I started washing dishes for a few hours every Saturday to earn some extra money. But mostly, I stayed home to give Papa much-needed help with the farm work.

That summer was the first time in decades that my mother wasn't in the field hoeing. Now, it was just Papa and me in the hot cornfield, hoeing what seemed like an endless number of rows covered with a jillion weeds.

I vividly recall one boiling-hot afternoon. There was no breeze for relief, and we moved slowly down the rows in the oppressive heat.

WORKING GIRL. Fourteen-year-old Myrtle Merton spent the summer of 1948 working the farm with her father to help the family make ends meet.

Just as we turned to make another round, Papa said, "Sister, I think we need to go to the house." When we reached the porch, the thermometer read 117 degrees.

Reaping the Harvest

My real test came when the tomatoes ripened. Mama said she'd pay me 10 cents a quart to can them. I soon learned what kind of work was in store for me.

I gathered the dusty, spiderweb-covered jars from the smokehouse and drew tons of water from the well to rinse off the dirt. I drew more water to heat and wash the jars with lye soap, then drew more for rinsing. My arms ached, but I was finally ready.

Toting a 10-gallon feed can, I hiked to the tomato patch. It looked solid red! Ripe tomatoes were everywhere. I couldn't believe how many there were.

I struggled up the hill to the house with the filled can. After drawing more water to wash the tomatoes, I peeled, cut and cooked them the way Mama had instructed.

When the tomatoes were ready, I filled each scalded jar and placed salt on top. The rubber on the caps had softened in hot water, which made for tight seals when I screwed on the caps and rings.

After canning all the tomatoes I'd gathered, I started the process over again. I usually did two batches per day. That summer, I canned 40 quarts!

When my mother saw the fruits of my labor, she praised my efforts and paid me what she'd promised—$4. I was so proud.

I've never forgotten the summer of 1948. Only after I became an adult did I realize how much my parents had struggled and how proud they were of me for helping.

Our lives were harder than I'd realized at the time. Yet, I believe I did what any farm girl would have done. It gives me great satisfaction to know I helped my parents when they needed it most.

It's not whether you get knocked down, it's whether you get up.

—Vince Lombardi

on the home front

THROUGH A CHILD'S EYES

I was just 6 when Pearl Harbor was bombed on Dec. 7, 1941. From that "day of infamy" until the end of the war, I witnessed the sacrifices and indomitable spirit of the folks at home.

Official national rationing—including the big ones, gasoline and meat—affected everyone. Gas wasn't a problem for my family because we didn't have a car until 1949. But those little red tokens for meat? There were never enough.

Seemingly everywhere I looked in my town of Medford, Massachusetts, I saw someone in a military uniform. Being an imaginative boy, I, too, wanted to wear a soldier's outfit. Thanks to a wealthy grandmother, I did get one!

And everywhere I looked, I saw a "V" for victory. There were victory bikes, victory stamps and war bonds. In school, I'd buy the stamps, lick them and put them in my stamp book.

My family kept a victory garden, too. One day, I was sent to my room for eating radishes right from the ground. Shortly afterward, my mother called for me. With moist eyes, she told me President Roosevelt had died. I was the only one she had that afternoon for support.

I was constantly involved with collections of paper, rubber...any item that could be sold so the money could be donated for the war effort. We even collected drippings from our bacon—when we could afford it!

In a food drive at the movie theater, we could receive a ticket for a can of food. At the time, a ticket was 10 cents. A can of peaches or Spam cost more, but donating food felt good.

In August of 1945, my family listened to President Truman speak about the bombing of Hiroshima. Germany had already surrendered, and in a matter of weeks, the war would be over.

I've never forgotten my childhood experiences from 1941 to '45. As I look back now, I recall those years as the best of my youth—in no small part because I saw the best in all of us.

—*Kenneth Hale, Ocala, Florida*

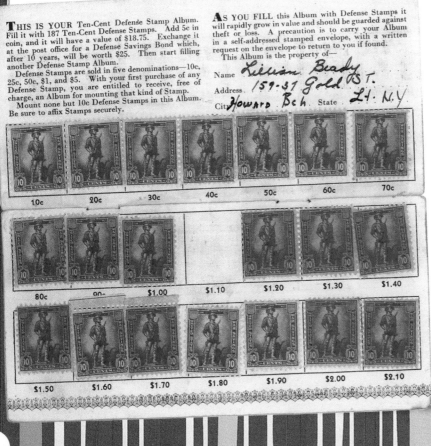

STAMP ALBUM. "I've saved these bond stamps since 1942, when citizens young and old were filled with patriotism," says Lillian Brady Clifford of Lynbrook, New York. "I can remember taking my 10-cent allowance and buying a defense stamp, eagerly waiting to reach $18.75, enough to convert it to a $25 bond payable in 10 years. Yes, even we children did our bit for the country with great pride."

PLANTING SEEDS. These Brighton Avenue School students in Atlantic City, New Jersey, joined in the war effort circa 1944. "I am the little girl with the straw hat and pigtails," says Helen Freas of Springfield, Pennsylvania. "The boy in front with me is Frank Wilson, who used to try to sneak the ends of my pigtails into an inkwell but never did succeed. Dorothy Mazeo is the girl reciting the message on the chart. Regretfully, I don't remember the other children's names."

JUGS FOR THE BIRDS

During World War II, city friends of my parents asked Dad if they could plant victory gardens on our farm near Rockford, Illinois. Dad left 1½ acres unplanted, and nine friends divided up the land into plots.

Most of the gardens looked very nice and did well the first year. One gardener, however, had a problem. His plot was located close to the fence line and trees, and he had trouble with birds continually pecking at the ripening crops.

That winter, he discussed this nuisance while at the office. His coworker jokingly suggested trying "whoo-whoo jugs." He said that if glass bottles were placed next to the rows, the wind blowing across the open necks would create a "whoo-whoo" noise and scare the birds away.

The next summer, six 5-gallon jugs were placed strategically in the garden along the fence line. I don't know if many birds were scared away, but the birds that made nests next to two of the jugs raised a fine bunch of youngsters!

—*Ed Johns, Pecatonica, Illinois*

Building a Newspaper
From the Mud Up

A HALF-BURIED PRESS MADE HEADLINES FOR THIS FAMILY—TWICE.

By Joyce Richards Case, New Iberia, Louisiana

When a hurricane raced toward the Texas coast in 1919, the small community of Taft was in the direct path of the storm. Winds exceeding 100 mph and tides that rose 16 feet above normal devastated the area.

Hurricane-force winds picked up the huge Cranston printing press from the building that housed the town newspaper, *The Texas Ranch Review*. The two-ton machine was carried away and hurled into a cotton patch, where it sunk into the muddy earth.

Before the storm, the sisters who owned the newspaper were on the brink of discontinuing publication. The paper had been limping along because there were few businesses in the area, and the local cowpokes were not avid readers.

Thinking the press had disintegrated in the storm, the sisters were downright slack-jawed when a farmer came into town and reported the Cranston's whereabouts.

When they saw the machine embedded in the ground 2 miles from town, they walked away, leaving it to rest it peace. *The Texas Ranch Review* was never re-established.

Out of the Mud

Two years later, my father, Henry Richards, was a young printer searching for a job. While visiting some friends in Corpus Christi, he met W. S. Clark, who was interested in starting a newspaper in Taft.

Dad agreed to join Mr. Clark in his venture. But first, they needed to find a location and buy equipment.

Folks around Taft told them about a printing press they could have for free if they were willing to retrieve it. This sounded too good to be true, but Dad and Mr. Clark followed directions and found the rusty machine sticking out of the ground.

The situation was almost laughable. Even if the press could be dredged up, how could it possibly be restored to running condition? But Dad never shied away from a challenge, and Mr. Clark was just as determined.

They rented a building in town to house the mud-clogged giant and gathered a crew of workers, plus mules, crowbars, shovels and two-by-fours. Somehow, they managed to exhume the press from its resting place.

After the crew completely dismantled the press, they rebuilt it from the ground up. The bed, ink trays, gears, rods, nuts and bolts were laid on the cement floor, and each piece was cleaned and oiled. Only the rubber ink rollers had to be replaced.

The shiny, good-as-new printing press was born again and christened "Big Black Bertha." On May 5, 1921—also Dad's 29th birthday—the first issue of *The Taft Tribune* was printed and distributed.

With Mr. Clark, Dad gave the business his best effort. But in the end, the town still proved too small to support a newspaper. *The Taft Tribune* was discontinued, and Dad moved on to work at other printing companies in the region.

Back to Bertha

Dad married my mother, Ida Davis, in 1928, and they established a print shop in Woodsboro, where they published the town newspaper. Our family resided in the small living quarters in the back of the building.

In 1942, two decades after Dad left Taft, another hurricane hit the Texas coast. Woodsboro was pounded by the wind and rain.

AFTER THE STORM. In 1942, Joyce Richards was too young to understand that her family had narrowly escaped a devastating storm. This photo of Joyce and her father was taken shortly after the hurricane hit the Texas coast.

IN PRINT. Joyce's mother, Ida Richards (right), is shown working with an employee in 1946 inside *The Taft Tribune* building. The Richards Printing Company took over the business in 1942.

Just after midnight on Aug. 30, we huddled inside while the whole building shook. When the telephone operator in the brick building across the street saw a piece of our roof fly off, she called and told Dad to bring us over.

I was just 10 months old at the time. Dad picked me up and guided my mom and two brothers to the telephone building and safety.

In the light of dawn, Mom and Dad stepped through the rubble that used to be their home and livelihood. There was little to salvage, and they decided to start fresh elsewhere.

While we were staying at a boarding house, Dad found out that an established newspaper in a nearby town was for sale due to the owner's declining health. That newspaper was—you guessed it—*The Taft Tribune*.

Dad obtained a small loan to launch the Richards Printing Company. From 1942 to 1950, the Richards family printed *The Taft Tribune* on a Cranston printing press named Big Black Bertha…the very one Dad had rescued from a cotton field 20 years earlier.

LOST AND FOUND. The building that housed *The Taft Tribune* was owned by the Henry Richards family in Taft, Texas, from 1942 to 1950. Henry had started the newspaper decades before.

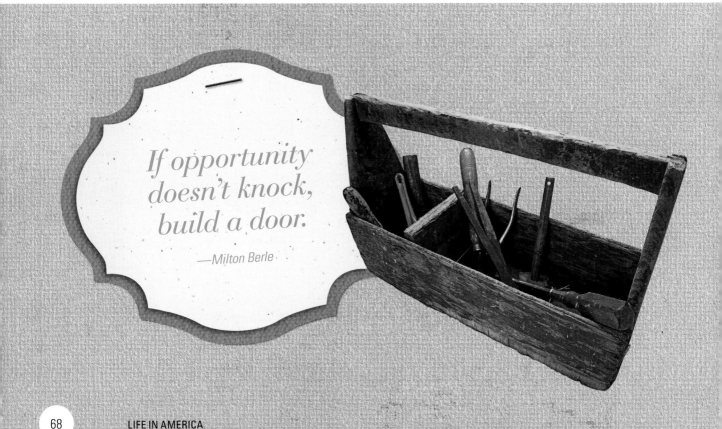

If opportunity doesn't knock, build a door.

—Milton Berle

doing their part

Lenore Rawls and her 8-year-old daughter proved a patriotic pair as they sold war stamps in a booth in Lewiston, Idaho, during World War II.

"My mother wanted us to look our best and made us matching outfits," remembers Janette Rawls Wilber of Boise, Idaho. "They were inspired by a *Ladies Home Journal* magazine cover from May 1942.

"I still have the cute little jumper I was wearing in this photo, which was published in our newspaper, *The Lewiston Tribune*."

the American DREAM

page 89

page 90

page 78

page 72

The Statue of Liberty welcomed weary immigrants to America's shores. From there, new citizens realized the dream of life in America…with plenty of ingenuity and hard work along the way.

"After coming through Ellis Island, my father worked in the iron ore mines of northern Minnesota until he could afford a small farm of his own," says Arnold Okerman of Littleton, Colorado.

"He and fellow Scandinavians soon built a new Scandinavia, with farmhouses like those they'd left behind. They cleared the timber, and my father donated the wood for a new school, where both children and adults could learn the language of their new land.

"The Scandinavian people had a stern morality. But they also enjoyed community fish fries and dances. And they believed this was a great land of opportunity.

"My wife once overhead my mother saying that when she first came to the United States, she thought the streets were paved with gold. 'And,' Mom added, 'they really were.'"

For these tired but hopeful travelers to a new land, the American dream really did come true.

Our Great Adventure to America

AFTER FLEEING NAZI GERMANY IN 1935, BUILDING A NEW LIFE IN RURAL PENNSYLVANIA WAS A WELCOME CHALLENGE.

By Lillian Claunch, Des Moines, Washington

It was 1935 when my mother, my older brother Conrad and I embarked on an ocean voyage to flee Nazi Germany. I was just 6 years old.

Our German mother had married a Jewish man from America. Father had been studying music in our town of Lübeck when the two of them met and fell in love.

Terrible stories had reached us about the treatment of Jews in the big cities. So Father wasted no time going back to America to ask relatives for money for our voyage. It was the Great Depression, though, and few people were able to help.

Meanwhile, the Nazis had invaded and taken over our town. They raised the swastika over the courthouse and searched every home, looking for weapons.

We narrowly escaped arrest when the Nazis discovered my father's checker papers with moves on the checkerboard written in numbers. They thought the numbers were a code until a neighbor explained what they really were.

We waited anxiously for word from Father, and the money finally came from our wonderful Aunt Sophie. We were joyous, yet it was a sad day when we had to say goodbye to our dear grandmother in Germany.

Trip Filled with Discoveries

For 9-year-old Conrad and me, the ocean voyage was a great adventure. Mama stayed in the room, seasick, while we ran all over the ship. We found pretzels in the bar and stuffed ourselves with these new treats. We also learned to play pingpong and lost many balls overboard.

One morning Mama woke us early and took us up on deck. "I'm going to show you something I want you never to forget," she said.

And there, in the distance, barely visible through the mist, was a most beautiful sight— the Statue of Liberty! To this day, I've never forgotten that emotional moment.

Grandfather and Papa greeted us in New York with a rattly Model T Ford and the happy news that we had a house in Applebachsville,

Pennsylvania. (We later learned Grandfather had won the house in a poker game!)

Home Was a Shock

After many flat tires, we finally arrived at the tiny village. We were directed to a narrow lane that would end at an abandoned 500-acre farm, our new home.

The lane turned into two ruts, and branches scratched the sides of the car as we bumped our way through the thick, dark forest.

Homesick, I closed my eyes and thought of the neatly scrubbed houses of Lübeck with their colorful window boxes.

The house was a two-story gray clapboard, shabby and empty, with a couple of broken windows. There was a huge tree in the front yard, a broken swing hanging from one limb.

A long porch ran along the front of the house and was framed by a skinny log railing. As we climbed the stairs, we heard yammering and spitting noises from under the porch. To my delight, several wild cats came running out, taking cover in the bushes.

Papa put his arms around Mama, and I looked up to see tears in her eyes. We opened the scarred, creaky door of the farmhouse and entered our new life.

Traded with Neighbors

Our safety net was Father's pension of $34 a month for being wounded in World War I. A few times, he won change playing against eager checker cronies at the general store.

Grandfather left us bags of old clothes to use and trade. Mama made quilts to use in that drafty house, and I think it was purely out of kindness that our Quaker neighbors gave us eggs and chickens for the strange items.

In the fall, Conrad and I went to a one-room schoolhouse in the village. There were six rows, one per grade, and poor Conrad had to sit at one of the small desks in the first-grade row with me until he learned English better.

After school, Conrad insisted we take the long way home through pastures instead of through the village with the other kids. I was afraid of the pasture, where a bull glared at us.

Sure enough, one time he charged at us. I was so petrified, I couldn't get over the fence quickly enough. Conrad's brave ranting and arm-flailing turned the bull away. I later told everyone at school, and Conrad became a hero. We never took the long way home again.

Father insisted on speaking only English at home, so we learned fast. On one unforgettable day, we found out there was a raise in Papa's pension, retroactive to January. We danced around the rooms, giddy with joy, even Papa.

Soon we were all at the village auction, although Conrad and I were more interested in the ice chest containing bottles of pop. We bought a lime rickey, and it tasted like heaven.

Meanwhile, our parents bought a winter coat for Mama and, wonder of wonders, a windup Victrola and one record—a polka. We danced to that record and sang all through the Depression.

Did we ever think we were poor? Never!

Give me your tired,
your poor

Your huddled masses
yearning to breathe free

The wretched refuse of
your teeming shore

Send these, the homeless,
tempest-tossed to me,

I lift my lamp beside the
golden door!

—Emma Lazarus
(Inscribed on the Statue of Liberty)

BOUNTIFUL HARVEST

As a wise man once said, "I don't care if you eat 'em or throw 'em, just as long as you buy my tomatoes."

As you can see, there were plenty of tomatoes and other items for sale on this produce wagon in 1914. The proud owner of the farm and wagon was Henry Smalle, the man standing in the center of the photo.

"My father, Adrian DeJaeger, is seated on top of the wagon," says Edward DeJaeger of Farmington, New York, who shared this photo. "He was only 14 at the time and had just come to this country from Belgium. Back then, Dad's family lived near the Smalle farm, and it was customary to let the children hire out to earn some extra money. The farm was located at Coldwater, New York, which is near Rochester.

"Also shown in the photograph are Henry's wife, the couple's children and the farm's hired man, who is holding the team of horses."

Judging from the looks of all those tomatoes, cauliflowers and other vegetables the Smalles were offering for sale, 1914 must have been a plentiful and prosperous year for their farm.

waiting for their ship to come in

A SUDDEN ILLNESS TOOK THE WIND OUT OF REFUGEES' PLAN TO SAIL TO AMERICA.

By Anna Smela, Schenectady, New York

We were living in Germany in 1952 when my husband lost his job as a journalist.

Being refugees from the Czech Republic, and with another job prospect virtually nonexistent, the only choice we had was to go to a refugee camp with our 5-year-old son, Misha.

A week later, our friend Tona stopped by. "Hello, you Americans. How are you?"

My eyes must have told him, "No jokes, please," but he laughed again and said with twinkling eyes, "Your visa came. We are sailing from Bramen on August 15."

The dream of many refugees at that time, a new permanent home in America, was to come true for us—and at a time like this. It seemed God was really on our side.

Our family left Munich for the refugee camp in Lesum. The afternoon of our arrival, we took the train into Bramen and spent the last of our money on shopping.

An Upsetting Delay

Shortly after we returned to our barracks at Lesum, Misha began to complain of an upset stomach and headache. *It's too much excitement,* I thought.

As I put Misha to bed, he tried to speak but couldn't get the words out. Suddenly, his body stiffened and he had a violent convulsion. The frightening attack lasted only a second, but the Polish women who were sharing our room ran to get my husband.

An American doctor gave Misha a careful examination. He then explained that because of Misha's seizure, we would need permission from the American consul in Bramen to emigrate, but the consul was taking a three-week vacation.

As night fell, the sounds of laughter and singing came from the street. Lots of Germans were celebrating the last night in their homeland before sailing to America. The next morning, the boat left port and the camp was deserted. Never had we felt so lost.

Life in the hospital where Misha stayed was comfortable. One day, a huge man appeared at the door of our room. Without any greeting, he said, "You no go to America? Your boy crazy in the head?" I was so startled, I couldn't answer. I later learned that he was an unfortunate like us, a Russian refugee whose son had a high fever.

Other occupants of the hospital included four Italian children whose mother had died and whose father was in Canada. The oldest was Victor, who was 6, and the youngest was 11-month-old Vera, whom I loved immediately. I held Vera in my arms and Victor gave me an approving look, but he became jealous when I brought my son in. I can see now how desperately he wanted my affection.

One morning the Italian children left to begin their long journey to Canada, and the time came for my husband to visit the consul. Sympathetic and kind, the consul promised to do everything in his power to approve our emigration. A test was arranged for Misha in the next two weeks.

August had gone by and September was waning when we made our final visit to the consulate. The doctor found Misha bright, intelligent and, best of all, ready to emigrate.

Authorities secured three berths for us on the *Groote Beer* ocean liner of the Holland/America Line. We sailed from Rotterdam, Holland, on Sept. 22 and arrived in New York City on a golden afternoon, Oct. 2.

Living in America

Misha, or Michael, quickly adjusted to his new life in America and spoke English within the first six months of school. At age 11, he appeared on the television show *The $64,000 Question*. His topic was baseball, and he won $16,000.

Misha married, had a daughter and lives in Michigan. He controls his neurological disorder with medication.

My husband, Michael Sr., and I initially worked as cleaners at the United Nations. I stopped work in 1956 when my daughter, Jane, was born, and my husband got into the hotel business. He eventually became manager of the St. Regis Hotel in New York City.

Michael Sr. died in 1976 at the age of 55, and I started work at Bloomingdale's, where I retired after 17 years.

I eventually moved to upstate New York to be close to my daughter and her husband, watching their three children while they worked. That was truly the happiest time of my life.

Despite many ups and downs, we have proven ourselves to be good, hardworking Americans, and I believe our American consul in Germany would not be disappointed in us.

I wish I could thank him for allowing us to emigrate and let him know that every time I hear *America the Beautiful*, it brings tears to my eyes.

NEW HOMELAND.
In 1952, the dream of going to America came true for Michael and Anna Smela (right) and their son Misha (opposite, far left). Their departure from a refugee camp had been delayed when Misha became ill.

One-Stop Shopping and a Goat

We called my grandparents, Samuel and Clara Sommers, by the Yiddish words for grandfather and grandmother, Zayde and Bubbe. After coming from Austria to the United States in 1902, Zayde looked for work as a tailor, but he couldn't find a job in his trade.

To support his growing family, he rented a pushcart and worked as a huckster, a common occupation on South Street in Philadelphia in those days. He was a well-respected merchant and served as treasurer for one of the benevolent associations formed to support members.

In time, he rented a store and became a greengrocer. Bubbe worked with him, and the children helped after school and on weekends.

The store next to Zayde's was a butcher shop. Zayde and the butcher became good friends and convinced the landlord to create an opening in the wall between the shops. This would allow customers to buy meat, fruits and vegetables—food for an entire meal—with the convenience of shopping at one location.

Today this kind of all-in-one convenience is taken for granted, but back then it was unusual. The connected stores gave customers an easier way to buy necessities, especially in bad weather, and more space to move around.

I have only vague recollections of the two shops themselves, but I have an extremely vivid memory of our store's "garbage disposal." To get rid of spoiled produce, which was a problem before air-conditioning, Zayde bought a goat.

He kept the animal in the dirt-floored storage room in the back of the store. The problem was, that nanny was mean. In fact, she was so bad-tempered that I was allowed to go to the lavatory next to the storage room only if an adult walked me there.

The goat remained until she butted Bubbe, the hand that fed her. That was the final straw. The nanny was sent to greener pastures—a farm.

The garbage disposal in my grandparents' store may have come and gone, but the friendship between the greengrocer and the butcher lasted until they retired.

—*Linda Abby Fein, Philadelphia, Pennsylvania*

the voyage over

TOURING NEW YORK

I came from Germany to the United States in 1947 aboard the *Ernie Pyle* (left). It took 10 days to cross the Atlantic, and when we finally saw the Statue of Liberty, it was a beautiful sight.

As a teenager, I was an avid tourist to the city's many attractions. I went to the top of the Statue of Liberty and the Empire State Building. What a sight the city was from the observation deck!

I will always cherish the day I came to the United States of America and New York City. Those were special times.

—Livia Greeson
Marietta, Georgia

A TERRIFYING TRIP

To get the money for my grandmother's second-class fare to America, her father sold a cartload of potatoes. Constance Bandurski made the voyage from Poland in 1913, when she was 16.

On the way over, her ship caught fire, and the passengers had to be transferred to another ship. I can't imagine how terrified this young Polish girl must have been, trying to understand what the English crew was saying as the fire raged.

My grandmother said there were cheers when they pulled into the harbor and got their first view of their new land. When she saw the Statue of Liberty, Grandmother said she thought it was the statue of a saint.

—Charlene Kowalski, Davison, Michigan

OFF WITH THE OLD

My grandparents Katherine and John Aufrecht came to the United States from Bergheim, Germany, in the 1800s. They had two young children, Fred, 2, and Lena, a babe in arms.

They said Fred was almost washed overboard when a big wave hit the ship. He was saved when a man grabbed him.

My grandmother told this story about their arrival: "What do you think was the first thing John did when we got to the new country? He threw his good German hat into the water and bought a new 'Yankee Doodle' one."

This thrifty woman never forgot what she considered to be a very foolish act!

—Josephine Dunn, Newark Valley, New York

Copr. 1955 Hunt Foods, Inc.

Oh, Mamma Mia!..wait till you taste
Pizza...made with *Hunt's* Tomato Paste

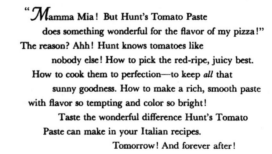

"*M*amma Mia! But Hunt's Tomato Paste
does something wonderful for the flavor of my pizza!"
The reason? Ahh! Hunt knows tomatoes like
nobody else! How to pick the red-ripe, juicy best.
How to cook them to perfection—to keep *all* that
sunny goodness. How to make a rich, smooth paste
with flavor so tempting and color so bright!
Taste the wonderful difference Hunt's Tomato
Paste can make in your Italian recipes.
Tomorrow! And forever after!

...the paste with the Sunny Italian Flavor **Hunt-for the best**

FREE! *Send for folder of best-loved Italian recipes. Hunt Foods, Inc., Fullerton, California*

Scarlet Fever Delayed Trip

EXPOSURE TO ILLNESS BROUGHT HER JOURNEY TO AN ABRUPT HALT.

By June Vezey, Wilsonville, Oregon

In 1910, my mother, Tina Johnson (at left in the photo below), came to the U.S. from Norway, via Canada. Her destination was Glendive, Montana, and a ranch where her two brothers were working.

When she reached Canada, her confidence began to waver, because a female German immigrant was found to have scarlet fever.

The woman was detained, although her sister and child were allowed to continue. The two rode on the same train car as Mother.

When the train reached Green Bay, Wisconsin, the child was diagnosed with scarlet fever. The car was sidetracked and quarantined, along with the adjoining train cars.

Mother's apprehension grew as she realized there was no way to get word to her brothers that her train's arrival had been delayed.

After two weeks, all the passengers appeared healthy, so they were allowed to continue their journey. But Mother's worst fears were realized when she finally arrived in Glendive in the middle of the night.

There was no one to meet her and no friendly policeman to ask for help. My mother surveyed the people around her and saw what looked like a Scandinavian face.

The man turned out to be a Norwegian who knew her family. He took my mother to a boardinghouse and promised to come for her the following day and take her to her family's ranch.

When morning came, Mother and the man were walking down the street when they happened to meet her brother Chris.

He had been coming to meet the train every night for two weeks, but the night before, he'd given up and gone to bed.

When they arrived at the ranch, there was an overdue—but very happy—reunion.

international call linked hearts

CONNECTING AN AMERICAN IMMIGRANT WITH HIS 99-YEAR-OLD MOTHER OVERSEAS REQUIRED A COW, CONSUL, CART AND CASH.

By Frances Erb, Pittsburgh, Pennsylvania

My grandmother, Frances Humel, was celebrating her 99th birthday in Czechoslovakia in 1945. My father had not seen her since he immigrated to the United States in 1907.

His parents had chosen to send four of their sons to live in the United States before they reached their 18th birthdays. At 18, they would have been eligible to be drafted into the Austro-Hungarian army.

Dad wanted to return to Czechoslovakia for a visit, but every time he planned a trip, fate stepped in and the money was needed for something else.

This bothered me. It seemed important that Dad, living in Pennsylvania, should have contact with his mother.

At that time, Europe was in turmoil. An individual telephone call was almost impossible. I was a young married woman with some free time on my hands when I had the bright idea to have Dad call his mother and wish her a happy 99th birthday.

I headed to the Bell Telephone office in downtown Pittsburgh and asked how I could place a call to my grandmother. I was told to write the Czech consul in New York City, which I did.

The consul called and told me the only place an international call could be received was at the mayor's office in Plzen, located south of my grandmother's village. He asked that I send him two certified checks—one in the amount of $150 for the mayor and another in the amount of $10 for the clerk who would monitor the call.

Grandma Was Thrilled

Dad wrote to his mother, telling her he wanted to call her for her birthday and asking if she could get to the mayor's office to take the call. Grandma wrote that she would be there and that she would be thrilled to hear her son's voice.

HELLO, PLZEN! Frances Humel drove a cart 18 miles to get a phone call from her son in Pennsylvania in 1945.

I returned to the Bell Telephone office to arrange for this special call.

Grandma lived outside of town, about 18 miles from the mayor's office. There was no transportation and, at age 99, she could not walk that distance.

She had a milk cart, but no pony. She did have several milk cows that she'd managed to hold onto during the war. She decided Daisy, the biggest and most docile, could pull the cart.

Grandma hitched up Daisy and started practicing with her every day, getting ready for the big trip. She figured it would take her two days each way, so she packed food for herself, fodder for Daisy and a large can of water.

She put a feather bed, pillows and clothes for herself in the cart. In a small purse pinned to her blouse, she had some money and her letter to the mayor. She was ready.

Most of the road was level, and she got along well the first day. There was no traffic to excite the cow, and Grandma sometimes walked alongside.

When evening storm clouds appeared, she asked a farmer if she could stay in his barn. The farmer said the cow could stay in his barn, but that Grandma would be the family's guest and stay in a fine bed. He refused money, and said he expected her to stop at the farm on the way back as well.

The next morning dawned bright and clear. Grandma expected to get to the mayor's office in about four hours. She began to wonder where she would put Daisy and the cart so they'd be safe.

By then, word had spread that a 99-year-old woman was on her way into town to receive a call from America. When she neared the town, a delegation met her. A police officer took charge of the cow and cart while the mayor's car took her to his office.

She Was a Celebrity

The building was decorated with bunting, flags and a sign that read, "Welcome, Frances Hausmann Humel!" A buffet had been arranged and was ready for everyone to enjoy lunch.

The mayor answered the phone. "Mrs. Humel is right here. Mrs. Humel, this call is for you."

At our home, where we had been waiting, the phone finally rang. The international operator put the call through, and Dad jumped up to answer it with tears in his eyes.

"Is that you, Frank?"

"MAMA!"

"Frank, Frank, Frank, Frank."

"Mama, Mama, Mama."

"Frank, Frank, Frank."

"Mama, Mama, Mama."

That went on for three minutes as tears streamed down Dad's face. Then the operator interrupted; their time was up. They never had a conversation! They were too filled with emotion to find words to say, but they didn't need them. The sound of their voices was all that mattered.

Grandma made the journey home with no problems. The trip was the highlight of her life. She'd celebrated her 99th birthday in style.

She never made it to her 100th. She died in her sleep about six months later. But she'd heard her son's voice one last time, and Dad was so grateful he'd had the chance to talk with his mother.

SERVING PROUDLY. Joseph Nemecek (shown in his Army uniform) learned some English, but his European style of writing numbers led to a longer enlistment than he intended.

Learning Language

BY THE NUMBERS

After coming to America from Czechoslovakia in 1913, our dad, Joseph Nemecek, found only menial labor because of the language barrier. He decided to take a night class in English.

In the first class, he learned a sentence, "Today is a fine day." The next morning, he quit his job of loading railroad wheels onto flatcars.

On his way home, Father passed an Army recruitment office. He went in, and the first question asked of him was whether he could speak and read English.

He said he could. As luck would have it, he was asked to read the very same sentence he'd learned the night before: "Today is a fine day."

Father then filled out the recruitment papers, which asked how long he wanted to serve. He wrote "1," meaning one year, but he wrote it in the European style and it was misinterpreted as "7." He found this out when, after a year, he asked for his discharge.

Father ended up serving in Mexico under General Pershing. He was wounded and eventually discharged.

With money for his education provided by his Army service, he became an engineer and spent the next 32 years designing streetcars for the Chicago Surface Lines.

He said he never regretted his "1" mistake.

—*Frances Pogwizd and Joseph Nemecek*
Machesney Park, Illinois

ENGLISH ONLY. "My mother, Angeline Huck (right), attended a German Lutheran elementary school in Chicago and graduated with her confirmation class in 1924," writes Charles Grizzle of Spokane, Washington. "My grandparents were German immigrants. My grandfather Reinhold Huck was a well-known butcher in Chicago. The family attended church services in German. But after the attack on Pearl Harbor, they stopped speaking German, even at home."

915 ½ SLOVENSKÝ AMERICKÝ SOKOL ♦ 915

AN ENDURING EDUCATION. This 1929 photo was taken at the Slovak school Amelia Weber and her sister Bess attended in Chicago. The girls learned grammar, history and other subjects.

HOLDING ON TO THEIR HERITAGE

My Slovak parents came to America from Europe in the early 1900s. It was important to both Mom and Dad that their children honor their heritage.

My mother and father settled in Chicago among people of Polish, German and Slovak backgrounds. When my oldest sister, Bess, and I started school, we did not know a word of English. When we grew older, my parents wanted us to remember the Slovak language and sent us to a Slovak school twice a week.

We started with the primer, learned some songs and later advanced to grammar, history and other subjects. Our teachers at the school included two sisters who also helped put on shows and danced.

The school, at 915 Willard Court in Chicago, was about 1½ miles from our home. We walked there not only for our lessons but also twice a week for gymnastics classes.

The education paid off. In 1965, my husband and I traveled to the region that is now Slovakia and met many cousins. I have no regrets about learning Slovak, as I still correspond with my family.

We had many fun times, and I can thank my parents for encouraging us to keep up with the Slovak language.

—*Amelia Weber, Port Richey, Florida*

Uncle Went From Riches To Rags...and Back

Many members of my family came to the United States in search of the American dream and to join Danish relatives here. They were proud to be Americans and never taught me the Danish language, though I heard it spoken throughout my childhood.

Some came as farmers, some as factory workers and one as a missionary to the immigrant Danes in the North, where many Scandinavians settled.

Grandma's cousin Anna, quite a beauty in her day, married an important Danish official, Fred Hauberg. He spoke German, Russian, French and English fluently and held a diplomatic position in Denmark.

Fred and Anna went to Racine, Wisconsin, before the turn of the last century. His first job was working for the Pugh Coal Co.—though not in the way he'd envisioned.

Hoping for an office position, he went to apply for a job there dressed in his formal diplomatic attire. He looked impressive in an embroidered vest, swallowtail coat, pinstripe pants, spats and top hat. But the boss, embarrassed, said the only job available was shoveling coal.

Fred responded, "Fine, I'll take it!" The boss handed him a shovel, and out he went to shovel coal dressed in his finest clothes.

He wasn't too proud to take the job, although it greatly distressed Anna. The rest of us were very proud of Uncle Fred for being a real American who wasn't afraid of hard work.

Later, Fred worked as a salesman with J.I. Case Plow Works in Racine and traveled all over the world, thanks to his language skills. He went from riches to rags and back again.

Like Fred, the rest of us found our way in our new country. Dad went from working in a factory to owning a tool-and-die business, and then took a job in Los Alamos, New Mexico, to serve his country.

Grandpa grew up on a farm and then started a funeral business. And my first job was working for the government as a grade-school teacher on an Apache reservation.

We all prospered in our adopted homeland and were very proud to be Americans, no matter where it led us.

—*Robert Ove, Rio Rancho, New Mexico*

Farewell, England

This photo was taken in 1914, shortly before my two brothers and I said goodbye to Grandma and left Nottingham, England, to sail to the New World. I wish I could remember the name of the ship we sailed on.

Note the Nottingham lace on our velvet suits; Mother worked in a lace mill. And how about those haircuts? We could be mistaken for the original Three Stooges! I'm the good-looking one in the middle.

— *Claude Wyer*
Farmington Hills, Michigan

The future belongs to those who believe in the beauty of their dreams.

—Eleanor Roosevelt

Fate Brought Grandparents Together

By Louise Concetta LaMarca-Gay
Rochester, New Hampshire

As a child, I loved listening to Dad tell the story of how my Italian grandfather and grandmother, Giacomo LaMarca and Concetta Ulyotta, met while searching for the American dream.

Giacomo was born in 1869 in Villarosa, a small village in Sicily. His family owned a great deal of land. Concetta was born in 1882 in the same area, but the two never met while in their homeland.

Several of Giacomo's brothers left Italy and settled in Ohio. Concetta didn't know anyone in the U.S., but she had seen posters advertising moneymaking opportunities in America.

When Giacomo decided to leave Italy, he sold his property rights to his remaining brother there. The money he gained from the transaction allowed him to make the voyage to America in first-class accommodations.

Lost and Found

Giacomo played the bass violin, which he brought with him on the trip. After a while, he became bored with the inactivity in first class. He noticed that steerage, where the poorest passengers were, was much livelier.

He went down to steerage with his bass violin and joined other passengers playing instruments. Concetta was traveling in steerage, and this is where they first met.

But after arriving in America and passing through Ellis Island, the two went separate ways. Giacomo worked for construction companies, while Concetta found a job in a shoe shop in Haverhill, Massachusetts.

After a while, Giacomo began looking for other employment and ended up finding a job in Haverhill. As fate would have it, the job was at the store where Concetta worked!

The two realized they had met on their way to America. And this time, they didn't part ways. They married a short time later.

The newlywed couple settled in Maine and eventually had three daughters and four sons, including my father. I'm named after my uncle Louie and my grandmother.

Since Dad passed away, I've missed hearing him tell my grandparents' story. But my name is a permanent reminder that I'm here because of their American dream.

From Columbia to
New Horizons

By José Zuluaga, Canóvanas, Puerto Rico

Growing up in a large, poor family in a small city in Colombia, I always considered the prospect of going to the United States to be a distant dream.

But thanks to the generosity of many people in Westfield, New York, my dream became a reality in 1967. An AFS scholarship gave me the opportunity to become a foreign exchange student in the U.S.

It meant I could attend school there during my senior year, 1967-'68. It also allowed me to live with host families who opened not only their homes but their hearts to me.

I first lived with Joseph Baideme and his family, then stayed with the family of George Rubin. Everyone was extremely kind to me and made my exchange student experience the most rewarding and significant of my life.

For the senior trip of my class at Westfield Academy and Central School, I was lucky enough to visit Montreal, Ottawa and Quebec. At the end of the year, I traveled with fellow AFS students to Massachusetts, Pennsylvania, Ohio, Florida and Washington, D.C.

Taking advantage of my exposure to English in the U.S., I acquired an excellent command of the language. It has given me a tremendous advantage in the workforce and broadened my horizons by allowing me to read many fascinating English books and magazines.

I have lived in the U.S. Territory of Puerto Rico since 1973, and in 1993 I became a U.S. citizen. Since my experience as an exchange student, I have visited the U.S. seven times and have maintained close contact with my host families and others.

I have such deep feelings of gratitude toward the United States. I love my native country of Colombia, of course—it's my homeland. But to be honest, I owe the U.S. a lot more.

Railroad from Mexico to U.S.

Before I was born, my father worked for the railroad in Mexico City. But he had bigger dreams for his family.

In July 1927, my parents left Mexico and arrived in El Paso, Texas, with their two young children in search of a better life. Father applied for a job at Southern Pacific Railroad but was rejected because he couldn't speak English.

He kept looking for work until he was hired in a garage to repair cars. In the two years he was there, he saved enough money to open his own garage, specializing in electrical systems.

His business thrived from 1929 until 1940, when two government agents came and told Father he'd have to close his garage because the copper, zinc and other materials he used were needed for the war effort.

The agents asked if he had other skills, and Father told them about his time on the railroad in Mexico. The government got him a job with the Southern Pacific Railroad, where his experience brought him a top salary. He worked there for 30 years before retiring in 1970.

My siblings and I thrived in our new country. My sister, Gloria, married an Air Force captain and had three children. My brother Lauro served in the Navy and graduated from the University of Texas at El Paso with the help of the GI Bill.

Another brother, Fernando, lied about his age in order to join the Navy when he was 15 and served for four years. He had six children and ran a successful appliance business. Sadly, he and his teenage son died in a plane crash.

I attended college for a few years, then worked for a large mortgage company and later started my own mortgage business. I thank God every day for guiding my father to the United States.

—*Horace Del Valle, Las Vegas, Nevada*

FAMILY TIES. Horace Del Valle is shown as an infant with his father, Severo, and brother Fernando (top), and at age 11 with his mother, Herlinda, and Fernando.

TRAVELING IN STYLE. The author (second from left) donned his sailor suit for an outing with (from left) his brother Lauro, cousin Rosa and sister Gloria. "My father worked hard to provide for our family," Horace says. "We were very lucky and experienced few hardships, even during the Great Depression."

family legacy

"This photo shows my father, Enrique 'Henry' Zappalorti, in front of his stained-glass and mirror shop in Brooklyn in the late 1920s," says Elaine Paralusz of Clearwater, Florida. "His father was a skilled glazier from Genoa, Italy, and taught his sons the business."

Hard at WORK

page 110

page 106

page 97

page 112

From mom-and-pop stores to Wall Street, American businesses were the foundations on which enterprising Americans built their lives. Heading out every morning for an honest day's work meant more than just a paycheck—it meant pride.

"Like so many men in eastern Kentucky, my father left the tobacco patches not long after World War I and went to work for the Louisville and Nashville Railroad," relates Paul Caywood of Evansville, Indiana.

"By 1928, Dad held the position of gang foreman in the bridge and building department. As a foreman, he was in charge of a crew and entitled to a train car for his personal use. So, for 9 years, our family of five lived together in a train car, traveling from state to state, without having to pay rent.

"My three siblings and I thought this life on the railroad was a real adventure. Our living quarters were far from fancy or modern. But it's how we rode out the Great Depression and stayed together as a family while Dad provided for us."

Turn the page for more stories of hardworking Americans carving out a living and a life…

Dad Was 'The Cracker Man'

POP'S JOB AS A TRAVELING SALESMAN WAS ALL IT WAS CRACKED UP TO BE—AND MUCH MORE.

By Danny Atchley, Mineral Wells, Texas

You could say I grew up on a Lance truck. I even came home from the hospital as a newborn baby in one of the company's trucks!

My dad, Vernon Atchley, was a traveling salesman for Lance, Inc. from the 1930s to the 1960s, selling crackers and other snack foods. He started his career in Paris, Texas.

While working his route, he was in a little store where my mother was running the cash register. They were married in 1941, and I came along in 1948.

World War II postponed Dad's sales career.

By 1948, however, he and his cousin Dave Baldwin were wheeling and dealing new customers for Lance all over Texas, Oklahoma, Arkansas and Louisiana.

Store owners would later recall how these two salesmen came into a store. One started talking while the other set up a display stand—and off they would go before the owner even knew what he'd bought!

I remember that Lance had interesting names for their products, such as Big Town Cakes, Toast Chee, Nip Chee, Van-O-Lunch Cookies and Choc-O-Lunch Cookies. Many

WHO'S HUNGRY? Snack time was prime time for Vernon Atchley (in the photo at left). A salesman for Lance, Inc. from the 1930s to the 1960s, he sold crackers and other munchies throughout Texas, Oklahoma, Arkansas and Louisiana.

of these products are still around today.

Their foods were great, but occasionally my sister and I would bring home a snack made by Tom's or Planters. (At that time, Lance made peanuts, too, a big item.) Dad would laugh at our purchase of a competitor's product and say, "You know better than that!"

On the Road Again

Thanks to Lance, I was an experienced traveler by the ripe old age of six. Dad took Mom and me from our Dallas home to many small towns all over his four-state sales region. We would stay in what were then called motor courts, where Mom had a kitchen and cooked our dinners.

I got my first haircut in a barbershop in a town called Opelousas, Louisiana. Dad liked to tell of the time we were snowed in for three days in Brownwood, Texas. And Mom always remembered a motor court in Ruston, Louisiana, where she heard singer

Kay Starr performing her hit song *Wheel of Fortune* in a honky-tonk next door.

My sister and I have fond memories of spending one week every summer in the 1950s in Mount Pleasant, Texas, at the Gaddis Motel and eating at the Alps Cafe. Mom would take us to a movie and the park during the day, and we'd all get in the pool in the evening.

In other towns, we would look for an Alamo Plaza, which was a nice chain of motels then. I always loved them because they were modeled after the Alamo, and the 1950s were the time of Davy Crockett and Fess Parker.

Our greatest Lance trip was in the

VIEWS IN ROCK CITY GARDENS

[TY] GARDENS   LOOKOUT MOUNTAIN

Don't Fail to see the Wonders in Beautiful Rock City Gardens.
DRIVE YOUR OWN CAR AND FOLLOW HIGHWAY 58, THE EASILY DRIVEN SCENIC HIGHWAY UP
LOOKOUT MOUNTAIN. YOU DON'T NEED A GUIDE AND ROCK CITY HAS NO ROAD-SIDE SOLICITORS.

ON THE GO. Vernon Atchley (at left in the photo at left) brought his family to Rock City Gardens in Tennessee and many other memorable places.

summer of 1960. Each year Dad had to fly to Charlotte, North Carolina, to attend business meetings, but that year he decided to make it a family road trip. We'd spend one week visiting places along the way.

Our first stop was Vicksburg, Mississippi, where we saw the Mississippi River and the city's Civil War battlefield. One day, we stayed in a fancy hotel in Jackson and ate breakfast in the dining room. The tuxedoed waiters, white tablecloths, and perfect ham and eggs will live in my memory forever.

South Carolina led us to more battlefields—the Revolutionary War sites of Kings Mountain and Cowpens. We also saw the huge carving of Confederate generals in Stone Mountain in Georgia.

I fell in love with Gatlinburg, Tennessee, which I thought was one of the most beautiful places anywhere. The Great Smoky Mountains were a real thrill. Mom was terrified of the height and the bears we spotted along the road, but we made it through OK!

In Chattanooga, Tennessee, we went to Rock City Gardens and Lookout Mountain. The drive up and down the mountain gave poor Mom another fright, as you could see the valley far below, and she just knew we were going over the edge at any moment.

Touring the Shiloh battlefield was emotional for us because our ancestors had lived in the area during the Civil War. I grew up listening to stories about how they could hear cannons firing day and night for nearly three days.

You can guess where we wanted to go in Memphis! There were plenty of fans at the gates of Graceland hoping for a glimpse of Elvis, but I'm sure he was off filming a movie.

Our last stop was Little Rock, Arkansas, so Mom and Dad could show us where we lived when we were very young. Then it was back to Texas and home.

With all of the places Lance crackers took me as a kid, I'll always love their products and be thankful for the many memories they gave me. And I'm glad they're still around!

Out on the Farm

NEWEST FARMHAND. This photo of grandfather and grandson, hand in hand around 1966, has special significance for Leo Graber of Marion, South Dakota. "My dad, Jonath F. Graber, whom I farmed with, decided to go check on the cattle or take care of a chore," he says. "My son Kendall, about age 2, took Grandpa's hand and walked out with him on his errand. I was born in 1928 and have many wonderful memories of growing up on the family farm."

FIELD WORK. "My dad, Jim Dailey, is shown here in the mid-1940s after he returned from World War II," relates Floyd Dailey of Cleveland, Ohio. "Dad was just outside of Sweetwater, Tennessee, taking a wagonload of tobacco to the barn to be cured. He worked very hard all his life and was well respected by all who knew him."

FORGING A CAREER. "Blacksmith work, a business of the past, was very necessary to a farming community," notes Edwin Dolezal of New Braunfels, Texas. "The man pictured in this 1950s photo is my father, Tom Dolezal, who owned and operated a blacksmith shop for 36 years in the little town of Shiner."

lots in store

GROCERS AND CUSTOMERS BUILT A SENSE OF COMMUNITY TOGETHER.

By Dorothy Wall, Oceanside, California

As I reminisce back to when I was 17 years old, my scene opens in a small neighborhood grocery store in Los Angeles, California.

I began working at the store in 1944, when our country was involved in World War II.

Blue rationing stamps were for kitchen staples in short supply, like sugar and coffee. Red stamps were for purchases in the meat department.

Each family member had a book of stamps, and if the total value of a stamp was not used, blue and red tokens were given in change.

Because of the shortages, the weekly arrival of a truck from the warehouse was anticipated like the appearance of a celebrity. By the time the loaded truck pulled into the parking lot, the store was so full of customers that you could hardly make your way from the back to the checkout counters.

Famous "Everyday" Items

The star attractions on that day were a pack of cigarettes, half a dozen eggs, one roll of toilet tissue and a cube of butter per customer, until the next week.

You could have taken the census on delivery day because all of the neighborhood families were represented. The lines at the checkout counter wound around the store. In those days, we ground coffee into a box or bag at the check stand.

Even though this store was part of a grocery chain, it really seemed to be just a neighborhood store. I took my afternoon newspaper from the son of a customer, and every St. Patrick's Day an

elderly man brought us shamrocks he had grown.

A woman who lived across the street from the store was a caterer. When she had leftovers from a catered meal, she gave them to us for lunch.

I relied on her cooking skills on the day I got married, too. She baked our wedding cake.

One woman crocheted rugs and another baked fruitcakes, both of which we were given at Christmas. When I was expecting my first child, a neighbor gave me a baby shower.

Our salaries were calculated on payday and given in cash in a brown envelope. Store hours were from 9 a.m. to 6 p.m. Monday through Saturday. Besides Sunday, we were given one other day off during the week.

The day the war ended, the main office called on our pay phone to announce the news. Our manager closed the store and told us all to go home. We were so excited. The meat department manager even came from behind his counter and kissed all the girls.

The streetcars were packed with people in a mood of celebration, and it was a noisy ride home. We were all eager to be with our families.

Even though many of the customers' names are gone from my memory, I can still picture many of the faces. Although it was a needed job, it meant far more to me.

THE FAMILY BUSINESS. "This photo of my grandfather John Hartman (in the doorway) was taken at the turn of the 20th century in Spirit Lake, Iowa," says Carlyle Parsons of North Liberty. "He is pictured with his wife, Cora; sons Milo, Imre and Carlyle; daughter Adelia; and friends of the family. Note the hitching post visible along Main Street. My grandfather's favorite slogan was 'You can buy the same thing cheaper at Hartman's.'"

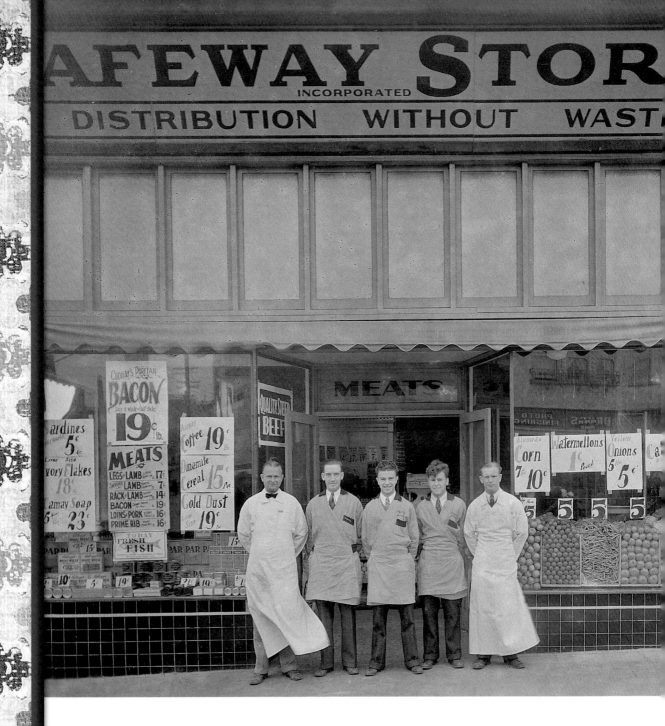

DISTRIBUTION WITHOUT WASTE!

That upstanding motto of Safeway stores is one I remember well. My father, Marty, worked for a Safeway in San Francisco.

Dad is in the center of the five men pictured in this photograph from 1932. It shows the fresh produce carefully stacked and arranged in the front window so it would be visible to passers-by. My father was quite artistic, and it was his job to create the displays and put up the signs that would draw customers' attention.

I think it's interesting to see what the prices were during the time of the Great Depression. You sure could eat well for the price, buying a leg of lamb for 17 cents per pound or prime rib for 16 cents per pound. In those days, 17 cents meant a lot more than it does now.

The photo also shows some of the brand names that were popular at the time, such as Underwood Sardines, Ivory Flakes, Camay Soap, Cudahy's Puritan Bacon, Dina-Mite cereal, Alameda corn and Gravenstein apples.

—*Diane Graves, Santa Rosa, California*

ALL-NIGHT SERVICE

My father, Amos Adams, was a druggist at
Lunney's Drug Store in Seneca, South Carolina.
This photo shows Dad at the store's grand
reopening after it was remodeled in 1954.

My older brother and I were young kids
during World War II, but we remembered the
knocks on the front door in the early-morning
hours. Someone would say, "Doc! Wake up,
Doc! I need a prescription filled!"

Because we didn't have a car at the time,
Dad would ride with the person the few blocks
to the store.

One time, a man came to our house and got
Dad out of bed to fill a prescription at 3 o'clock
in the morning. While at the store, the man
asked to buy an ice cream cone.

Dad, who was normally a very patient and
accommodating person, told the man very
bluntly, "The fountain is closed!"

—*David Adams, Lithonia, Georgia*

*Opportunity is
missed by most people
because it is dressed
in overalls and looks
like work.*

—*Thomas Edison*

Space Program Job Was Heavenly

THE BEGINNING OF AMERICA'S RACE FOR SPACE WAS EXCITING AND MEMORABLE—EVEN FOR THOSE WHO NEVER LEFT EARTH.

By Diana Wilson Solomon, Sherman Oaks, California

To this day, I am proud to have been a small part of this country's space program during the five years I worked for Rocketdyne, beginning in 1958.

Rocketdyne, located in Canoga Park, California, was a division of North American Aviation, which later became Rockwell.

I was one of the receptionists in the lobby of the main administration building. We wore blue gabardine suits, white blouses and blue pumps—no slacks, of course. Our net pay was about $98 every two weeks.

My duties were to make sure guests were registered and given an identification badge. We also saw to it that they were properly announced and escorted, if necessary.

We greeted about 10,000 guests a month. Many of them were in tour groups for the military, mostly the Air Force, and people involved in the space industry. The general public was not allowed inside the building.

A Special Guest

Security was heavy in those days. When guests left, they had to return their badges, account for any material they took from the plant and have their departure recorded.

An exception was made once for famous aviation pioneer Charles Lindbergh—a tall, good-looking man with a shy and gentle smile. He received a customized badge with his name engraved on it.

When he and his entourage were about to leave, he removed his badge and handed it to me. I told him he could keep the badge as a souvenir, but he smiled, shook his head, handed me the badge and left.

SPACE STATION. A reception desk was the station for the author (center) and co-workers JoAnn Blough (left) and Callie Leftwich in 1961.

The badge was a "throwaway," made just for Lindbergh. So I decided to take it home as a souvenir and give it to my grandmother, who lived with us.

Grandma's eyes lit up when I gave her the badge. She couldn't believe that I had met the great Charles Lindbergh! I also met other famous visitors, including Jimmy Doolittle, Jimmy Stewart, Werner Von Braun and the first astronauts.

I'll never forget when those first astronauts rocketed into space, powered by a Rocketdyne Atlas missile. It was so exciting for everyone. And I was so thrilled to have been a small part of our country's space history.

Special Delivery

THAT'S A WRAP! "This group of paper boys was preparing to deliver *Newsday* in Freeport on Long Island in New York," relates Reverend Robert Murphy from Chester, Connecticut. The reverend is the Catholic priest at St. Joseph's Church in Chester. "I am in the center, in the light shirt. Seated around me, clockwise from far left, are Bob Furman, a boy whose name I can't remember, Ed Boyle, Arnold Plummer and Larry Wiley. This was in 1942, one of the first years for *Newsday*."

PROUD POSTMAN. "My father, John Keithley, looked handsome in his uniform as a mailman for the U.S. post office in Compton, California, where this picture was taken in 1932," says Anita Wewers of Kansas City, Missouri. "Dad later transferred to Springfield, Missouri, where he retired in 1961." He apparently still had a lot to do, as he was just 10 days shy of 102 when he passed on in 2004.

Things may come to those who wait, but only the things left by those who hustle.

—Abraham Lincoln

Feeding the
FLAME

THE DREAM OF BEING A FIREMAN LIKE DAD SPARKED INTO REALITY—TWICE.

By Bob Teates, Bradenton, Florida

When I was about 10 years old, I had a lot of fun playing fireman because I wanted to be like my dad, Noble Teates, who was a Washington, D.C. firefighter.

I had a wooden wagon that Dad fixed up like a fire engine. It had a yard sprayer filled with water and a little push-button bicycle siren.

I even had an old fire helmet that Dad had salvaged from somewhere, so I felt like the real thing. And a couple of times as a boy, for brief periods, I got to be the real thing.

Dad worked just a few blocks from where we lived, and I used to ride my bicycle to visit him during the mid- to late 1930s.

The second floor of the firehouse had lots of beds in one big room. Sometimes, the firemen let me slide down the shiny brass pole from their bedroom through a hole down to the main floor.

While I visited Dad at the firehouse, the men often received a fire call. The "watch man" would ring a big bell several times and the men would all come running, don their boots, coats and helmets and, with red lights flashing and sirens blaring, ride the engines away to the fire.

Couldn't Believe It

One day, the fire station received a call to handle a small brush fire, and Dad asked me if I wanted to ride along. I was so excited, I didn't know what to do!

One of the firemen grabbed me and we jumped on the back of the lead fire truck. He held me close to keep me safe, between him and the back of the truck, sort of hidden away. Dad rode up front with the driver. I never will forget that ride with the flashing red lights and the wail of the siren.

Another thrill came a while later. On holidays and special occasions, the firemen would fix a big meal, but one man had to remain on watch.

On one of those days, I was asked to watch the desk while all of the firemen ate together. They figured nothing would happen during the short time they enjoyed their meal.

However, the phone did ring and I answered it. A voice told me that the engines needed to respond to a trash fire. I wrote down the location and rang the big gong...boy, was it loud!

All the firemen came running and asked if I was sure of the location and the nature of the fire. I told them I was sure, and off they went.

I don't know who was more hopeful that the information was correct, the firemen or me.

In later years, after serving in the U.S. Navy, I joined the Washington, D.C. fire department, in the communications division. I became one of the "voices" from fire alarm headquarters.

One day, I received a report of a fire in Dad's district. I rang the emergency phone at the fire station, and Dad happened to answer with, "Engine 25, Truck 8, Captain Teates." I replied, "This is headquarters; for the engine and truck companies, respond to..." That was a proud moment for me, never to be forgotten.

LIKE FATHER, LIKE SON.
As a boy, Bob Teates visited his father's Washington, D.C. firehouse in the 1930s.

Pageant Was Part of Job

My dad, Joseph Krajewski, was a popular Rheingold beer salesman affectionately known as "Joe Rheingold." From about 1936 until 1963, he worked in the Sweezy Avenue Depot in Riverhead, New York, owned by the Liebmann Brothers and known as the Liebmann Breweries.

Dad was an enthusiastic promoter of Rheingold beer. During the days of the "Miss Rheingold" pageant, he had a lot of fun advertising the contests. Beer drinkers voted for their favorite pageant contestant, and the winner was featured as Miss Rheingold in advertisements.

I recall Dad bringing me autographed snapshots of each year's pageant winner. Sadly, I seem to have lost those pictures over the years.

This photo, taken in the summer of 1949, shows me in the center holding a cardboard ballot box for the 1950 Miss Rheingold contestants. I'm surrounded by my cousins, Marian Szczepanik Adler (left) and Felicia Szczepanik Paprocky (right).

—*Joanne Krajewski Doroska*
Riverhead, New York

THE SURVEYING CREW. Shown in this 1939 photo are (front row, from left) J. Karter, Don Whittemore and Paul Martin; (back row, from left) N. Broderick, O. Dugas, Jim Gateau, Charles Hardy, Joe Racicot, Amos Gagnon and the author.

CCC Camp Offered Both a Job and a Home

In 1939, I'd completed three years of high school in Livermore Falls, Maine, when my mother got sick, and I had no place to live.

I was 18 and, like thousands of young men, I decided to join the Civilian Conservation Corps. It was a good place to live. I was sent to the 130th Company at Alfred, Maine, where 200 of us were housed in four barracks.

On a typical day, I worked from 8 a.m. to 4 p.m. on a survey team relocating the boundaries for national forests. A Maine state forester served as our boss.

We were given work clothes, and the food was very good. We'd be driven into the woods to work, and they brought us a hot meal every day. We did the surveying, summer and winter.

From 4 p.m. until the next morning, we were under military jurisdiction. We had inspections, and they told us when to put out the lights in the barracks at night.

I worked in the CCC camp until 1941, when I heard about job openings with Pratt & Whitney in the aircraft industry and got a job there. Soon, I learned that I would be drafted for the war, so I enlisted…and ended up being stationed in Rhode Island. That wasn't what I thought or hoped would happen; I wanted to see the world.

—Roy Sherar, Haverhill, Massachusetts

OUT IN THE WOODS. The 130th Company, Alfred, Maine, was a typical Civilian Conservation Corps camp, complete with rec hall, mess hall, barracks and quarters for the officers.

Chop your own wood, and it will warm you twice.

—Henry Ford

the fall gather—
a cowboy story

By S. Gary Roberts, Austin, Texas

This story happened sort of this way, at least as I recollect it.

When my older brother and I (inset) were youngsters during the mid-1940s, our daddy would take us out of school in the fall for a couple of weeks to hire out as day help for our neighbors, the Laskeys, who were doing their fall gather.

We never referred to the fall gather as a roundup (that came from the movies), but that's basically what it was.

The foreman's name was Buck something, but we just called him Mr. Buck. To us young boys, it was a real treat to get to work with the real cowboys.

The Laskey ranch was a fair-sized one as places go in that part of west Texas. Seems like it was 10,000 to 12,000 acres, but that could have been just the south pasture. They mostly referred to size in those days as sections—one is 640 acres, or one square mile.

We had four horses that would take to the saddle or harness. Dad rode a horse and led one while we two boys each rode a horse. We were paid $1 a day for each of the horses and $1 a day for my brother and me.

Daddy was a good hand, so he drew $2. He was nearly 6 feet 3 inches tall and could do just about anything they needed done. All in all, Dad got paid $8 cash money a day for every day we got to work.

Being about 10, I mostly ran chores and kept the count on whatever we were splitting out or culling. I was proud of being the counter chosen by the foreman.

A Rocky Situation

Mr. Buck was very particular about keeping a clean count on which cattle went where. To make sure you didn't lose your place, you kept a pocketful of rocks.

If the bunch was small, you'd put a rock over in your other pocket every time five steers or heifers or yearlings came by. With a big herd, it would be every 10. When we finished the count, I'd hand the foreman my rocks and give him the number we were using.

The foreman or some of the other hands would send me off on wild goose chases, like running a mile run across the pasture for a saddle stretcher. The walk back, after I found out there was no such thing, felt a lot longer.

Another time, a good left-handed rope man they naturally called Lefty was missing a few of the skittish calves. Mr. Buck told me it might help Lefty if I'd ride my horse over to the main barn and get a left-handed rope.

Well, I jumped at the chance. The man at the barn seemed to know just what I needed.

I rode right up to Lefty, gave him the rope and told him what Mr. Buck had said. Lefty looked

GREENER PASTURES.
This crossing of the Dismal River in west-central Nebraska is typical of summer cattle movements before the fall gather. The photo is from Daniel M. King, Red Bluff, California.

sort of sour and accepted the new rope without saying a word, glancing around at the foreman. You know, I don't think he missed another calf the rest of the day.

Daddy got me thinking when he said I could probably put a stop to the "hoorawing" if I got back at them a bit. I thought that could make it either worse or better.

The next afternoon, at the end of a long day, Mr. Buck motioned for me to bring the counting rocks so he could mark the tally book. Just as I got close,

I held out both hands full of rocks and stubbed my toe, spilling the rocks everywhere.

Mr. Buck sucked in his breath and let out some words I hadn't even heard the hot-iron men use. He looked long and hard at the catch pasture, his shoulders sort of drooped, then looked back at me. I grinned and began to pull the right count out of my other front pocket.

You know, Mr. Buck never sent me on a wild goose chase again. He even called me by name instead of "Button" now and then.

Workin' on the Railroad

HARD LABOR. A section crew on the Chesapeake & Ohio Railroad in Russell, Kentucky, posed for this photo in 1929. "My father worked for the C&O Railroad for more than 30 years before retiring," relates Henrietta Cash of Amherst, Virgina. "Our family had some really hard times, but Dad was able to own his own house and farm. He was always a very hard worker." Her father, Henry Switzer, is shown seated, third from the right.

RIDING THE STORK SPECIAL

As a baggage master for the Milwaukee Road, my dad, Abe Weaver, earned the title "Midwife of Milwaukee" for an incident that occurred in 1920.

My father was on a run from Great Falls, Montana, to Harlowton when a passenger told him a woman was about to have a baby and there was no doctor on the train.

Dad had the woman moved to the baggage car. There, he set up trunks and boxes for a makeshift delivery table.

After the baby arrived, the mother asked my father his name. She said she wanted to name the infant after him.

Because his name was Abe and the baby was a girl, he suggested naming her Geraldine instead, after the next town they would be coming to.

As word of the birth spread through the train, passengers took up a collection to start a bank account for the baby. She and her mother were then whisked away to a hospital.

Many years later, in 1942, my father was sitting on his front porch when a young woman approached him and said, "Mr. Weaver, I'll bet you don't know who I am."

"I don't believe I know you, and I don't think I've ever seen you before," my surprised father admitted.

"My mother told me all about you. My name is Geraldine," the young woman said, "and I was born in a baggage car."

This brought back a wonderful memory for my father, who passed away a short time later.

—Dale Weaver, Eugene, Oregon

Mother Helped Atlanta's Ladies Look Their Best

My mother, Alma Alene Coleman, worked as a beauty operator for years at the S.A. Clayton Company hair salon on Hunter Street in Atlanta, Georgia.

The shop is no longer there, but during my mother's time, it catered to a wealthy clientele.

She gave permanents to ladies who sat under a machine with wires above them to get the curls they wanted. My mother also knew how to give finger waves and marcels, using a curling iron and the proper techniques.

She also was an expert manicurist. I still have her old-fashioned tools with their ivory handles (shown in the photo above right). She used files, cuticle pushers and nail buffers to make the ladies' nails shine.

Mother used to say that the backseat of her car was filled at Christmastime with nice gifts from the ladies for whom she had worked.

She married my dad, Roy Franklin Wright, in 1914, when she was 17. He died when I was only 9 months old, and my mother married my stepfather, Sam Van Wyke Pierce, in 1918.

My grandmother Kathryn Coleman took care of me while my mother was working as a beauty operator.

I returned to live with my mother when I

BEAUTY was the business of Alma Coleman (inset and second from right, above) using a manicurist's tools of the trade (right).

was 7 or 8 and completed my work at Commercial High School, as my mother had before me.

"Miss Alma," as she was affectionately known, was very active in the First Baptist Church in Red Oak.

Mother often had her pastor and friends over to our house for home-cooked meals, serving them vegetables from her garden and old-fashioned, melt-in-your-mouth corn bread she made from scratch.

When she passed away at age 93, I called her pastor, the Rev. Gene Boyd, and asked him to preach at her funeral.

He agreed, and this is where he met my youngest daughter, Dorothy. They fell in love and later married.

I felt sure that my mother, looking down on us, had arranged it all with God.

—*Evelyn Mitchell, Columbus, Georgia*

Jobs on the Home Front

By Jean Hayes-Bartlett, Rupert, Idaho

It was June of 1943, and Mom had left our home in Klamath Falls, Oregon, to stay with my sister in Portland when her first child was born. There, Mom learned that the shipyards needed workers.

She got a job for herself, then recruited me. I was 17 that summer and eligible for a job.

Mom knew a lady in Newburg who agreed to rent me a room and feed me. At that time, buses made round trips from Newberg, hauling employees to and from the shipyards every day.

Most of the jobs were for welders, and I had no experience. But it wasn't considered a problem because training was provided. I was outfitted with leather welding clothes, which consisted of overall-type pants, a long-sleeved jacket, gloves and a helmet.

I was able to master horizontal welding, but vertical proved a real challenge—and overhead seemed downright impossible! However, a team of shipfitters needed a welder to work with them on the Liberty ships they were building for the war effort, so off I went.

My job was to weld what was called a dog— a holding device used on hinged parts of the ship. Luckily, not one of the dogs I welded ever flew off, so I did have something to be proud of.

After I completed my welding, a professional followed to finish the job. Then the dogs were removed by a worker using a cutting torch.

We were warned to make sure our helmets were over our eyes before we touched metal with the welding rod. One day, thinking this step was unnecessary, I decided to bypass it.

I soon discovered there was a very good reason for protecting your eyes when an arc is set off in front of your face! I had to go to the infirmary for medication, and I spent my day off the next day taking care of my injured eyes.

I worked days, and I was lucky enough to witness the breaking of a champagne bottle across the bow of a Liberty ship as it slid down toward the Pacific Ocean.

My job ended when I returned for school in fall. But I've always been proud that my first job was on a Liberty ship. My maiden name of Jean Wheeler is listed in the archives of the World War II National Monument in Washington, D.C. as a worker on the home front.

From Ships to Trains

After I graduated from high school in the spring of 1944, Mom again began looking for employment possibilities. She decided I needed a job before starting college in September.

Mom was working in the Southern Pacific Railroad yards in Klamath Falls and heard they were hiring women to service trains passing through. She thought it would be a good job for her two teenage daughters, so off we went.

I don't recall a job interview; I think we just

IN THE SHIPYARD. Handbooks (left) containing safety tips and information for shipbuilders are souvenirs of the time Jean Hayes-Bartlett spent working in a Portland, Oregon, shipyard during World War II.

appeared for work. We were hired for the swing shift, from 3 p.m. to 11:30 p.m.

To get to work, my sister Janice and I had to walk about 2 miles to a bus stop and take a city bus into town. Dad drove to meet us at the bus stop when we returned, so we never had to walk home after dark.

Our job was to replenish the water and ice for trains in the Klamath Falls depot. To get the ice ready, we had to chip a 100-pound ice block into quarters using an ice pick and tote the 25-pound blocks to an ice cart.

It took two women to move the cart up the platform where the train's dining car would stop. A man climbed the ladder with the ice on his shoulders and dropped it into the holding tank on top of the car.

We also had to "spot" the hose carts along the platform to fill the water tanks on the side of the train. All of the tanks had to be filled on every train.

On my regular shift, we expected only one train each day, which arrived at about 10:55 p.m. After servicing it, we returned the carts to the little hut where we hung out between trains.

The spare time between trains was our "free time." We had to remain on the premises but could do just about anything we wanted—read, embroider, even sleep. It was a rather cushy job!

For the Troops

World War II was still raging that year, and troop trains came through Klamath Falls several times a week because it was on the main line from north to south. It was our job to service these extra trains as well.

The servicemen were not allowed off the trains, so they hung out at the windows, whistling at the pretty young girls and trying to get as many addresses as they could while we were doing our jobs.

Because I had just graduated from high school, I had a whole supply of calling cards with my name printed on them. So I wrote my mailing address on back of the cards and handed them out to the soldiers.

Being a normal teenager, I flirted with the troops and was happy to send friendly messages to cheer up lonely servicemen.

As a result of the cards, I was inundated with letters, and I answered every one. I even sent my own pin-up picture. I believe I got more mail that any other girl in college, and I never divulged my secret for having charmed so many servicemen!

Though I sent hundreds of these letters to servicemen, I ended up going on a blind date with only one of them. He drove to Klamath Falls from The Dalles, Oregon, to take me out.

PIN-UP GIRL. The author (shown here in her Sunday best in 1944) brightened the day for servicemen in World War II by mailing a pin-up picture with a friendly letter.

Jean Wheeler

DRESSED WITH CARE. Nursing student Doris Daumer (right) posed in her uniform while working at Haff Hospital in Northampton, Pennsylvania.

Dream of Nursing Nurtured a Career

By Doris Daumer, Northampton, Pennsylvania

Oh, to be a nurse! Ever since I was a young girl in grade school, I wanted to be one. Fortunately, that wish came true—and I was lucky enough to stay in my dream job for decades.

After my high school graduation in Allentown, Pennsylvania, in June of 1941, I entered nurses training at Haff Hospital, a small medical facility in Northampton. I was a graduate of the two-year practical nursing class of 1944.

At the time, nursing students wore a traditional uniform—dress, bib, apron, pinned-on collar and cuffs, white shoes, stockings and white cap. In cold weather, I also wore my nurse's cape. We looked very professional.

Nurses worked 12-hour shifts, beginning at either 7 a.m. or 7 p.m. Four students covered the hospital on the night shift, and six others worked during the day.

We were trained in many procedures of surgical medicine and maternity, and our patients received good care. Maternity patients usually remained in bed for nine days and went home on the 10th. Surgery patients and others remained at the hospital for one to two weeks, depending on the type of procedure.

Long Days, Long Nights

Student breakfast was held in the hospital's dining room at 6:30 a.m. sharp, starting with a reading of a Bible passage and the Lord's Prayer. Before the day shift began, we also were briefed on the reports from the night before.

Medicines were given, temperatures were taken and charting was done at assigned times. All patients received bed baths, and beds were changed every morning while patients remained in them. Patients also had no bathrooms, only urinals and bedpans.

The doctors on staff made their rounds every morning. When needed, the doctor who owned the hospital and his son were called in for medical emergencies.

Meals came from the kitchen on a cart in an elevator, and many patients had to be fed. After the noon meal, it was time for p.m. care—washing hands and faces, combing hair and getting patients ready for visitors. Visiting hours were 2 p.m. to 8 p.m. daily.

On Sundays, a minister and choir members from a local church would come and give a short service. They stood on the landing in the stairway, and all doors leading to the stairs were opened so patients could hear.

During the service, students had to mop patient rooms, dust and wash medicine glasses. On Sunday evenings, we cleaned and resupplied dressing carts. We also filled holders with alcohol to hold cleaned thermometers.

We had full schedules every day, but we adjusted to the demands of the job and truly enjoyed our work. I enjoyed nursing as much as anyone—I retired in 1985 after 40 years. I still think back fondly on those days, my fellow staff members and the patients we cared for.

right place, right time

Living near a busy intersection in 1939 Los Angeles led to my first business venture at the ripe old age of 11.

We lived three doors off the corner of 48th Street and Crenshaw Boulevard. There were bus and streetcar lines on Crenshaw and the end of a streetcar line on 48th.

My dad knew I wanted a bike in the worst way, so he suggested I sell soda pop on the corner that summer. Dad must have contacted the folks at Coca-Cola Bottling Co. because, by golly, a distributor stopped by the house with a cooler on wheels (shown above) and set me up in business.

They, along with employees from the Nehi soda company, would stop by each week to see what I needed.

Every morning, I loaded the cooler with pop and ice (thanks to the iceman) and rolled it down to the corner. That summer, I made enough money at 5 cents a bottle to buy myself a new bike.

It's hard to imagine a kid being able to do something like that today. Now you would need a retail license, liability insurance and a seller's permit and have to report to the franchise tax board. I miss those days of truly free enterprise.

—*Byron Martin, Angels Camp, California*

CHAPTER 6

Family VALUES

Life lessons from Mom, Dad, brothers, sisters and other relatives have not only shaped the people we've become, but also taught the value of family.

"My grandfather came to live with us in 1929, when he was 'old' to me and I was just 2," relates Nat Swann of Signal Mountain, Tennessee. "From that day on, he became my constant companion, confidant, teacher and best friend.

"Dad often had to be away overseeing the details of the farms he managed there in Pelham, North Carolina. So Grandfather took on the job of surrogate father to me. I called him 'Big Daddy.'

"He taught me so much about plants, animals, fishing and the constellations. I was delighted by the rides he gave me in the wheelbarrow and by the stories he told of his youth as we sat on the porch. For 12 years, he was the most important person in my life.

"Big Daddy passed away when I was a teenager. But I will never forget the love he so unselfishly gave and how much it meant to me."

Other folks share their own heartwarming family stories on the pages that follow...

page 121

page 137

page 123

page 131

'It's Just a Jar of Peaches'

MOM'S GENEROSITY AT THANKSGIVING DURING THE GREAT DEPRESSION WAS PAID BACK IN FULL—AND THEN SOME.

By Evelyn Smith, Charleston, West Virginia

My mother (pictured at right) had a lot of faith in God, which she truly needed in 1933. My sister was a baby, and I wasn't old enough to go to school. Dad had left us, and the Great Depression was at its worst. Mom took in washing to make a living.

Around that time, several missions for the poor sprang up in Charleston, West Virginia, where we lived. One was run by the Rev. Earl Hissom. He lived in a poor section of town and began preaching in an abandoned storefront, which grew into a church building with a ministry to the needy.

Eventually, Rev. Hissom (everyone called him Earl) could afford to air a radio program in the mornings, which Mom would turn on after she woke up my sister and me. His message was always one of hope.

On his program just before Thanksgiving, he asked for food donations to be set out so his truck could pick them up. Volunteers, he explained, would deliver food to the poorer sections of town the night before the holiday.

When my mother heard the request, she immediately strode into the kitchen, took a jar of home-canned peaches from the pantry and set it on the front porch for the truck to pick up.

The neighbors who saw this told Mom she was too poor to give away that jar of peaches. One, a particularly cynical woman, said Mom was "a fool for giving Earl Hissom anything." The woman said he was a crook and would either keep the peaches himself or sell them.

As a 4-year-old, I heard this and wondered myself if Mom was making a mistake.

But Mom held her ground, and the peaches stayed on the porch. She told everyone who advised her not to do it that she would give the peaches in good faith, and it was up to Earl what he did with them. "For heaven's sake," she said, "it's just a jar of peaches!"

They were picked up a few days before Thanksgiving, and we thought no more about it.

Truth Came as a Shock

On Thanksgiving Eve, as we were getting ready for bed, there was a knock on our door, and we heard footsteps quickly leaving.

STILL STANDING. "When I visited my childhood home (above) in later years, I remembered the spot on the porch where Mom left the peaches," says Evelyn Smith.

When Mom opened the door, she couldn't believe what she found. There was a box of food on the front porch.

We were overwhelmed. Mom had always stressed how much we had, not what we lacked, and taught us to thank the Lord for His blessings. We never expected that some kind person would bring us food, much less a big box of food for Thanksgiving!

Excited, we brought in the box and began to unpack the goodies. There was a freshly dressed chicken, some potatoes, dried beans, rice, flour, canned pumpkin and—you guessed it—the jar of peaches Mom had canned herself and donated to Earl for the less fortunate. She sat on the floor and cried.

I walked with her to the kitchen, and she carefully placed the jar of peaches back in the empty spot on the top shelf, where it had been just days before. It had come home, bringing other good things with it, and our family feasted on a delicious Thanksgiving dinner the next day.

"You can't outgive God," Mom said as she prepared our special holiday meal. "You reap what you sow."

My young mind saw the fruit of Mom's faith, and it made an indelible impression on me. She made sure the whole neighborhood knew about the goodness of the Lord, and after that, I never heard anyone call her a fool.

The best way to give advice to your children is to find out what they want and then advise them to do it.

—Harry S. Truman

NICE, BUT NO LEGROOM

To celebrate the widespread popularity of the 1965 Ford Mustang, each Ford manufacturing and assembly plant nationwide had employee drawings for Mustang pedal cars. The cars were also sold at dealerships for $12.95 and later at stores for $25.

My father, James Fleming, won this little Mustang at the plant in Ypsilanti, Michigan. In this photo, which ran in the Ypsilanti newspaper, Dad held the balloons as I tried to sit in the Mustang.

At 11 and "kinda big for my age," I found the car to be a tight fit. I can still hear my mom, Joan (standing in the doorway), laughing because I had a hard time keeping the front wheels on the ground when I sat in the car.

I may very well be the first person to have pulled a "wheelie" in a Ford Mustang.

—*Michael Fleming, Belleville, Michigan*

THE WALK STOPPED HERE

Going places with my Uncle Anthony was one of the best things about my childhood. He was a bachelor, a caregiver to his parents and a brakeman with the Pennsylvania Railroad, which entitled him to railroad passes.

We both enjoyed talking about American history. One summer afternoon in 1945, he called to ask if I would like to go to Washington, D.C., the following week.

It was the first time I'd seen the nation's capital, and we visited several sights, including the White House. Uncle Anthony suggested that we walk through a park opposite the White House. Then, from a distance, he thought he saw President Harry Truman; he knew the president took walks in the park.

Uncle Anthony quickly gave me his camera, telling me to snap a picture of the president.

I was fumbling with the camera, not sure how to use it, when I heard a voice call out, "You're too far away, son." The president motioned for me to come closer, and I walked toward him. When he was right in front of me,

he stopped, smiled, and, with a Secret Service man in the background, let me take his picture.

I thanked him, and he replied, "You're quite welcome, young man."

I'll always be grateful to my uncle for taking me on that eye-opening trip and giving me the opportunity to meet the president.

—*James Hughes, East Islip, New York*

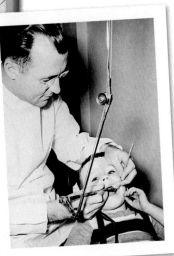

the flying
McKinleys

TO TAKE AN ACTIVE CLAN OF 13 ON FAMILY VACATIONS,
MOM AND DAD WENT TO EXTREME MEASURES.

By Gwen Francis, Houston, Texas

With 11 children, our family outgrew traditional modes of transportation in the 1960s, presenting unique problems for parents who loved to travel.

The McKinley clan was raised in Fraser, Michigan. Detroit later absorbed that municipality and retained little of its former distinction as a community, which had once revolved around the church, school and chocolate-dipped Dairy Queen cones.

My father, "Doc" McKinley (shown above with my brother Otis Lee), was the town dentist and, later on, its mayor. He built the first privately owned airport in Michigan, where he operated a Cessna dealership and flight school.

Our home was built between the east/west and north/south runways. This was Fraser's answer to the White House, although it was more utilitarian than grand. But it *was* white. Made of whitewashed concrete blocks, it was built to withstand a hurricane, even though we lived 1,500 miles inland. It did, however, withstand a whirlwind of children—five boys and six girls.

Daily chores included gathering eggs from the henhouse, feeding the horses, mowing the grass and washing mounds of clothes hung to dry with wooden clothespins that doubled as dolls, when given a little fabric.

Our active family spent summers cooking out, skiing, swimming and tirelessly assembling hammocks that stretched between trees rigged with clothesline and moth-eaten wool blankets.

With hammocks stacked one on top of the other, the bark soon gave way to the rope as the top hammock inched toward the next and so on, until the bottom hammock was filled with tangled blankets and children.

Unconventional Outings

We used an airplane for some vacations, and Dad often flew us up to our farm in Romeo four or five at a time. It was only a 15-minute flight from the runway next to our home to a grassy field on the farm.

Because of the size of our family, Dad also bought a Greyhound bus, removed the seats and installed a bathroom with a tub and shower, a 9-foot table, a refrigerator, a four-burner gas stove, a king-size bed and various bolted-down sofas and chairs.

Sleeping bags covered the floor at night, and by day, decks of cards, Archie comics, coloring books, jumbo crayons and children rocked and rolled across North America.

Mom plagued us all with matching plaid shirts and starched jeans when we filed out of the bus to sightsee, thereby ensuring it was our family that was the sight to see!

From the 1964 New York World's Fair to the Indian reservations of New Mexico, the "McKinley Flyer" was a novelty, generating enthusiasm for RV travel across America.

The idea worked so well that we eventually replaced it with a second bus, the "McKinley Flyer II."

Often interviewed by local media, Dad was once quoted as saying, "It cost $13 in diesel fuel to travel from Michigan to Washington, D.C. My parents believed travel was an education incomparable to the classroom.

Quality Time Together

We worked hard, played harder, laughed often and rarely missed church. Sunday mornings meant three hours' prep for a one-hour sermon. The girls donned ribbon-clad straw hats and white gloves, and the boys wiggled incessantly through church in starched white cotton shirts, razor-thin ties and ankle-length wool slacks belted just under their chins.

When we were not in school or traveling, we stayed busy dredging canals for home sites on Houghton Lake, assisting in the

*We **worked** hard, **played** harder, **laughed** often...*

dental office, trimming Scotch pines to sell at Christmas for $1 a foot, or tending cattle at the farm in Romeo.

The farm created the perfect setting for what would later become McKinley's Pine Valley Golf and Country Club. The family staffed the golf shop and snack bar, cut the fairways and orchestrated golf outings.

Together, Mom and Dad raised a family taught to value relationships and honor God. Our parents, who are no longer with us, left a legacy of 11 children and many grandchildren and great-grandchildren. I'm sure my siblings and I can never adequately express our appreciation for the commitment my parents made to our family.

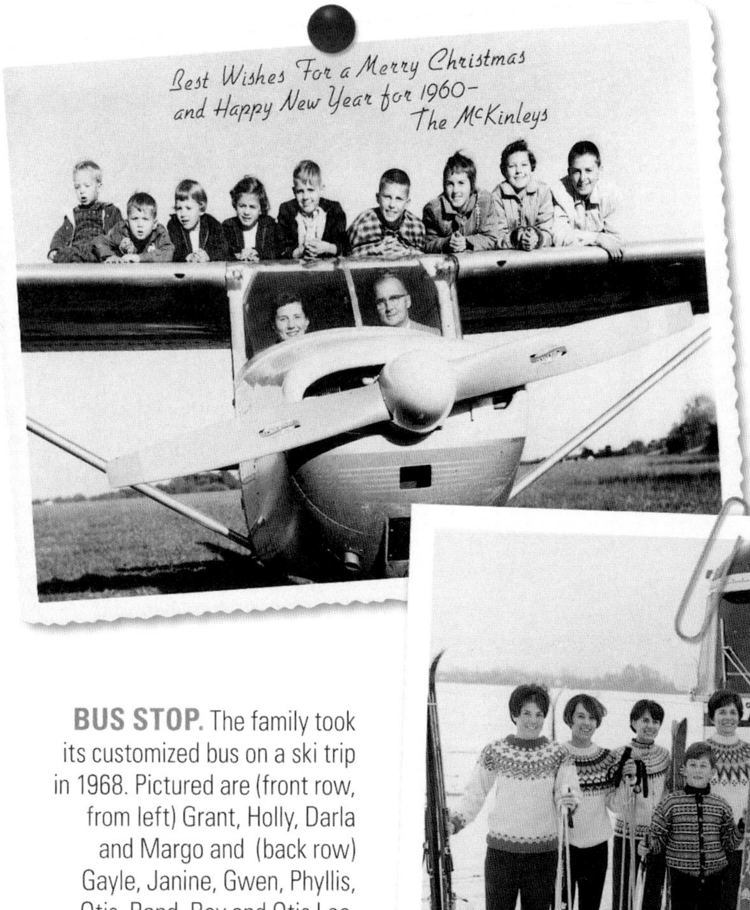

Best Wishes For a Merry Christmas and Happy New Year for 1960—The McKinleys

THE FLIGHT CREW. Phyllis and Otis McKinley had plenty of travel companions, including Bryan, Grant, Margo, Gwen, Rand, Ray, Janine, Gayle and Otis Lee, shown here in 1960.

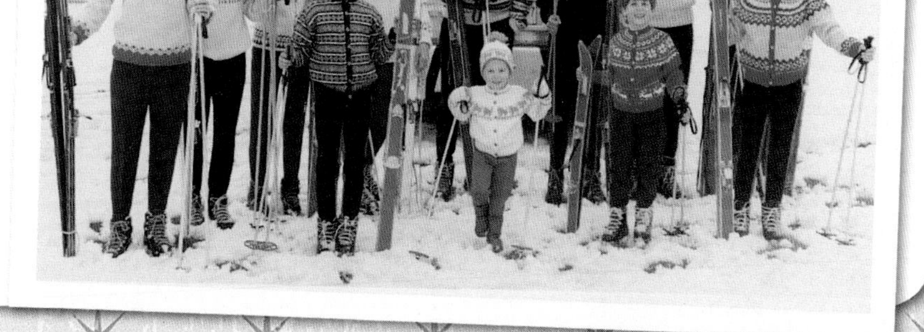

BUS STOP. The family took its customized bus on a ski trip in 1968. Pictured are (front row, from left) Grant, Holly, Darla and Margo and (back row) Gayle, Janine, Gwen, Phyllis, Otis, Rand, Ray and Otis Lee.

Earthly Angels Pay a Visit

DAD TAUGHT A CHRISTMAS LESSON NEVER TO BE FORGOTTEN.

By Charlene Elizabeth Baltimore, Scottsburg, Indiana

It was Christmas Eve 1949. I was 15 and feeling sad because there was not enough money to buy the dress I wanted. We did the chores early that night, so I figured Pa wanted extra time for us to read the Bible.

After supper, I took off my boots, stretched out by the fireplace and waited for Pa to start reading. I was still feeling sorry for myself and, to be honest, wasn't in much of a mood to listen to the Scriptures. But Pa didn't get the Bible; instead, he bundled up again and went outside. I couldn't figure it out—we had already done all the chores.

It was a cold, clear night, and there was ice in Pa's beard when he came back in. "Come on, Elizabeth," he said. "Bundle up. It's cold out."

I was upset. Not only wasn't I getting the dress, now Pa was dragging me out in the cold. I put on my coat and boots, and Ma gave me a mysterious smile as I opened the door. Something was up.

Outside, I became even more dismayed. There, in front of the house, was the work team, already hitched to the big sled. Whatever we were going to do wasn't going to be a quick job.

I reluctantly climbed up beside Pa, the cold already biting at me. We pulled in front of the woodshed, put on the high sideboards and started loading wood—the wood we spent all summer hauling down from the mountain and all fall sawing into blocks and splitting.

Finally, I asked, "Pa, what are you doing?"

"Have you been by the Widow Clark's lately?" he asked.

Mrs. Clark lived about 2 miles down the road from us. Her husband had passed away the year before, leaving her with three children to raise on her own.

"Yeah," I said. "Why?"

"I rode by just today," Pa said. "Little Jake was out digging around in the woodpile trying to find a few chips. They're out of wood, Elizabeth."

That was all he said, and we loaded the sled so high with wood that I began to wonder if the horses would be able to pull it.

The Spirit of Giving

Pa then went to the smokehouse and took down a big ham and a side of bacon, telling me to go load them. He returned to the sled carrying a sack of flour over his right shoulder and a smaller sack of something in his left hand.

"What's in the little sack?" I asked.

"Shoes. They're out of shoes. Little Jake had gunnysacks wrapped around his feet when he was out in the woodpile. I got the children a little candy, too. It just wouldn't be Christmas without some candy."

We rode the 2 miles to the Clarks' place in silence. I tried to think through what Pa was doing. We did have a big woodpile, meat and flour, so we could spare that, but I knew we didn't have any money. Widow Clark had closer neighbors than we did; why was it our concern?

We unloaded the wood behind the Clark house and knocked on the door. It opened a crack, and a timid voice said, "Who is it?"

"James Cotton, ma'am, and my daughter, Elizabeth. Could we come in for a bit?"

Mrs. Clark opened the door, and we went in. She had a blanket wrapped around her shoulders. The three children were huddled underneath another blanket, sitting in front of a small fire in the fireplace. Widow Clark fumbled with a match and lit the lamp.

"We brought you a few things, ma'am," Pa said and set the sack of flour and meat on the table. Pa handed her the other sack. She opened it hesitantly and took out the shoes, one pair at a time. There was a pair for her and one for each of the children—sturdy shoes that would last.

She bit her lower lip to keep it from trembling as tears filled her eyes and ran down her cheeks. She looked at Pa as if she wanted to say something, but it wouldn't come out.

"We brought a load of wood, too, Ma'am," Pa said. He turned to me and said, "Elizabeth, go bring in enough to last awhile. Let's get that fire roaring and heat this place up."

I wasn't the same person when I went to get the wood. I had a lump in my throat and tears in my eyes.

Soon, the fire was blazing, and everyone's spirits soared. The kids giggled when Pa handed them each a piece of candy, and Widow Clark looked on with a smile that probably hadn't crossed her face for a long time.

"God bless you," she said. "I know the Lord sent you. The children and I prayed that He would send one of his angels to spare us."

Pa insisted that everyone try on the shoes before we left. I was amazed when they all fit, and I wondered how he had known what sizes to get. Then I guessed that if he was on an errand for the Lord, the Lord made sure he got things right.

Pa took each of the kids in his big arms and gave them a hug. They clung to him and didn't want us to go. I could see that they missed their pa, and I was glad that I still had mine.

An Unforgettable Christmas

At the door, Pa turned to Widow Clark and said, "The missus wanted me to invite you and the children over for Christmas dinner tomorrow. The turkey will be more than the three of us can eat, and a man can get cantankerous if he has to eat turkey for too many meals.

"We'll be by to get you about 11. It'll be nice to have some little ones around again," he added.

With a look of deep gratitude, Widow Clark nodded and said, "Thank you, Brother Cotton. I don't have to say, 'May the Lord bless you.' I know for certain that He will."

On the sled, after we had gone a ways, Pa turned to me and explained that he and Ma had tucked away money here and there all year long to buy me a dress for Christmas.

Yesterday, when he had seen little Jake with his feet wrapped in gunnysacks, Pa knew what he had to do. "I spent that money on some shoes and a little candy for those children. I hope you understand," he said.

I understood very well. My father had given me a gift much greater than a dress. He gave me the look on Widow Clark's face, the smiles of her three children and the best Christmas memory of my life.

An Impromptu WEDDING

By Faye Adams, De Soto, Missouri

It was June 1954, and the Korean armistice had been in effect for less than a year. Skirmishes along the 38th parallel were frequent, and the uneasy truce between the North and South kept border patrols on the alert. The U.S. Air Force stood at the ready.

My husband-to-be, Bill, was in the Air Force and stationed in Great Falls, Montana. He was part of a fast deployment wing, designed to be able to set up operations anywhere in the world in just three weeks.

Bill and I had been engaged for 18 months, and our tentative wedding date in September was just a few months away.

Near the end of June, Bill called to tell me that he was being sent to Japan in September. The only airmen being granted leave were those getting married immediately and those who needed to attend a family member's funeral.

"Could we get married now?" Bill asked.

A quick wedding wasn't what I'd envisioned for us. But 10 long months had passed since his last leave. I didn't have the heart to say no.

Bill arrived in St. Louis, Missouri, on Sunday, July 4, and our plan was to exchange vows on Friday. Public offices were closed on Monday, which was the official holiday. On Tuesday, we rushed to apply for our marriage license and get the required blood tests.

We also had to buy my dress, wedding rings, flowers and a suit for Bill, who preferred not to be married in uniform. Mom ordered the wedding cake, and we asked Bill's uncle, a pastor in another town, to perform the ceremony.

What Could Go Wrong?

On Friday morning, we picked up our marriage license. When the time came to leave for our evening wedding, the flowers had not been delivered. With family in tow, we drove to the church without them, dressed for our nuptials.

En route, we got a flat tire. In the oppressive 104-degree heat, the guys had to take off their jackets, roll up their white sleeves and change it. The other women and I stood along the shoulder as cars whizzed by, stirring up dust and trash from the roadway.

We stopped at a florist and had some white carnations hurriedly arranged into corsages and a bridal bouquet. When we finally arrived at the church, almost an hour late, Bill's uncle said he'd thought we'd changed our minds and was about to close the church and go home.

After everything that had happened, our ceremony lasted less than five minutes. I thought, *That's it?* Our wedding had no people-packed pews, no dream dress, no photographer. I had a hard time believing I was a married woman.

We headed back to my parents' house for a short reception with cake and punch. Wouldn't you know, there were the lovely camellias we'd ordered for the wedding. They'd been delivered after we left for the church.

We hopped into my brother's 1953 Ford and headed off to Arkansas to visit Bill's family. Ten

days later, Bill was in Japan and I was back at my clerk/typist job at a St. Louis bank. I proudly wore the corsage of orchids that Bill had wired to me from his stopover in Hawaii.

After four lonely months, I boarded a train for a two-day ride to Montana. Finally, I would be joining my husband to begin our life together.

SPUR OF THE MOMENT. Bill and Faye Adams quickly married in July of 1954 when they learned Bill had to leave for Japan in September. "We had neither the time nor the funds to hire a photographer, so we didn't have any pictures taken of our wedding," Faye says. "The portrait above was taken at a studio in St. Louis, Missouri, a few days later."

1923

Wouldn't a *Wholesome* hot drink at breakfast make the day brighter~for everybody?

Your intuition tells you when there is the slightest change in the well-being of your loved ones.

How often you have wo whether coffee or tea was to for that indigestion, headach of "nerves"! Why not fin

Unlike coffee or tea, l Postum can be depended t a healthful drink—abso harmless, even for children. and old enjoy its delicious

and delightful aroma, and it has a "body" that is truly satisfying. Instant Postum is a wholesome

POSTUM

SO EASY TO MAKE

Merely pour boiling water on a level teaspoonful of the Instant Postum granules in a cup. Stir thoroughly; then add sugar and cream.

Your grocer also sells Postum Cereal (in packages) for those who prefer the flavor brought out by boiling fully 20 minutes.

The cost of either is about one-half cent a cup.

Sold by Grocers Everywhere

A WINTER DAY—
with a happy ending

1940

A soup that cheers you when you're cold!

When the snow drifts high and finger tips tingle, a plate of Campbell's Vegetable Soup is welcome indeed! Steaming and savory, it comforts you with its very look. Its invigorating, full-flavored beef stock is chock-full of nourishing garden vegetables—*fifteen different kinds.* Almost a meal in itself, Campbell's Vegetable Soup, mothers say, matches in good flavor the finest vegetable soup they can make at home. Keep it on hand, and enjoy it often!

LOOK FOR THE RED-AND-WHITE LABEL

A good steep hill,
Perhaps a spill;
Then Campbell's Soup,
The final thrill!

Campbell's
Vegetable Soup

CONTAINING 15 GARDEN VEGETABLES PLUS RICH BEEF STOCK

Skating Away Together

By James Martin
Fund du Lac, Wisconsin

I've always been proud of my parents…except for during those adolescent years when I realized I knew more than they did. To their credit, by the time I reached early adulthood, they had somehow become really smart again.

I'm most proud of my parents for the way they managed to make a lot out of, well, not very much. One of my favorite memories of childhood is the ice skating rink Mom and Dad created in the backyard of our Villa Park, Illinois, home.

Winter cold and snow seemed more dependable in those days. After the weather turned icy and a blanket of snow formed, Dad would clear an area of about 30 square feet and form snowbanks around the square on all sides.

Then, most mornings for several weeks, Mom would get out the hose and flood the area. Eventually, this created a nice, even patch of ice on which my parents, sister, brother and I could have all kinds of fun.

We skated to waltzes on the radio, played games of tag and crack the whip with neighbor kids and slid down the neat ice slide we formed down a snowbank. We even had winter picnics complete with hot cocoa.

I was starstruck by the skating abilities of my older sister, Lonnie, and older brother, Bobby. Once, Lonnie announced proudly, "I can skate with one foot in the air." I confirmed enthusiastically, "At *least* one!"

Another time, Bobby somehow convinced Lonnie she could go even faster if she left the rubber blade guards on her skates. So she left them on and gave it a try. She didn't gain speed, but she did take a spectacular nosedive into the ice!

The last winter for our rink was unusually long, so Mom had plenty of time to get the ice really thick. We had great skating conditions all the way into April. When most kids had already caught spring fever and started tossing around baseballs, I was still saying, "Hey, wanna come over and skate?"

Finally, at the end of April, the ice was gone—and so was the grass underneath. Who knew that putrefied sod could smell so bad? That's when I was introduced to a rototiller.

'Lulu' won her heart

By Lee Stratford, South Jordan, Utah

I had about a month before I needed to head back to Brigham Young University to finish my college education. It was August of 1949, and I had just returned to Lomita, California, after serving two years as a missionary for the Mormon Church.

During that month, friends from high school invited me to dinner. While at the couple's apartment, I commented on a 1923 Model T Ford I saw in the parking lot. I was shocked when my friend Marvin asked, "Would you like to have it?"

Having just returned from working as a missionary, I had no money. But with my dad's help, I bought the car from Marvin for $10.

The snazzy black sedan was in great shape. In preparation for the winter in Utah, I had a new roof put on for $20. I also painted the hubcaps red and the wooden wheel spokes white and blue in honor of my service in the Air Force during World War II. The rear and back side windows had Venetian blinds.

I named my Model T Lulu and frequently crooned the song lyric, "Little Lulu, I love you, Lu, just the same" from the *Little Lulu* comic strip.

Arriving on the BYU campus, I gained immediate notoriety for my unusual old-time car. I couldn't get in it without seeing people pointing and smiling. They especially loved the "oogah" horn and cranking start.

Mobile Matchmaker

The very best thing about Lulu was her captivation of the cute girl I was dating. Betty "Liz" Martini fell in love with Lulu first, then Lulu's owner.

I met Liz at a vaudeville show one evening at BYU. Three girls performed a pantomime, and for some reason, I felt in my heart that I would marry one of those girls. It didn't take long before I knew it would be Liz.

I drove Lulu to pick up Liz for basketball games, movies and whatever else was going on. We wrote slogans on Lulu (like those shown in the photo below) and used her as a "campaign chariot" when Liz ran for junior class secretary. And it was in Lulu that we had our first kiss.

When Lulu needed repairs, I got a job on the graveyard shift as a laborer to pay the bill. Between work and classes, I got only four hours of sleep each night—and ended up dropping one full grade in each of my classes.

But when the bill was paid, I could look forward to a fresh start with the next quarter in school. And more importantly, I could get back to spending time with Liz!

Lulu had become a part of me, but I knew I'd eventually have to sell her. We drove to Liz' house one day in the spring of 1950, and that was the last time Liz sat in Lulu.

I'll always love Lulu for helping me meet many people at BYU and for bringing me on many fun road trips. But, most of all, I'll love her for helping me capture the heart of my girl.

Liz and I graduated from BYU on June 2, 1952. We got married the next day and enjoyed 36 wonderful years together.

FUELED BY LOVE.
In the photograph at left, Lee Stratford and Liz Martini attend a dinner dance in 1951. The couple married a year later and went on to have seven children and many grandchilden and great-grandchildren.

CAR ATTRACTION.
When the author (left) had his Model T repaired at a Ford dealership, the dealer used this photo to advertise his safety contest.

Onnie Was Like a Mother

By Virginia Rowe, Lebanon, Ohio

I was 10 days old when my mother died and my father sent me to live with "Uncle" Frank Crosier and his wife, "Onnie," in Lebanon, Ohio.

They weren't my aunt and uncle; Onnie was a distant relative. Onnie's first name was Annice, but Onnie was as close as I could get in my younger years. They were an older couple but proved to be a wonderful choice to care for me.

I was born prematurely. Uncle Frank, a kindhearted physician who had served during the Spanish-American War, nursed me along. I weighed just 10 pounds at 5 months, but nourished by Uncle Frank's formula of oats, lime and milk, I began to gain weight and thrive.

Tough Days Ahead

Onnie struggled with a painful affliction. She suffered severe arthritis stemming from a bicycle accident in the early 1900s.

Then, during the Great Depression in 1933, Uncle Frank passed away. Onnie was left with a little insurance money and a big building that had been a sanitarium, but now held apartments.

Money was scarce. At times, tenants did the laundry or cleaned for us. More than once, their rent went unpaid.

Tenants were never forced to move, though, and things somehow always worked out. One man even patched a hole in the building's tin roof using bandages left from Uncle Frank's practice that had been dipped in tar.

Onnie, who also had studied medicine, was a mentor to many of the families that lived in the building. She even delivered babies.

She was keen of mind and taught me household skills so well that I can still hand-sew a buttonhole that's better than one made by a sewing machine. I made my first dress on her treadle machine when I was in fifth grade.

JUST WHAT SHE NEEDED. "Onnie" Crosier (left) and Virginia Rowe share a special moment together in 1940.

But Onnie taught me much more than basic domestic skills. She raised me to appreciate all kinds of music and to read for the sheer enjoyment of it. I learned good English skills, polite manners, proper table etiquette and respect for my elders.

Freedom to Choose

Onnie sent me to Sunday school and church, but when I was old enough, I was given the choice and not forced into any of these activities.

She came from an interesting family. In the days of Walden Pond, her grandfather lived in New England and was a frequent visitor to the home of author Henry David Thoreau. Her grandfather was an abolitionist who helped with the Underground Railroad after moving to Ohio.

Onnie was not afraid of anyone or anything. Once, while she was counting the rent money at 1 a.m., a stranger approached from outside her window. Instead of panicking, she demanded to know who he was and what he wanted.

Most importantly, she loved me dearly and gave me the care I needed. She lived to see me marry and held my first child to her heart.

My mother was taken from me at a very early age, but Onnie was the next best thing. I was so fortunate that she and Uncle Frank took me in.

fathers truly knew best

My romance with my husband originated in a cemetery in Toms River, New Jersey, where our mothers are buried side by side.

One day, the two widowers were tending the graves. Their conversation led to details regarding their children, Frank and Florence.

According to Pop Clay, his son was interested only in boats and fishing. Pop Emond noted that his daughter would be a great homemaker.

An introduction was arranged on a Sunday. Frank had been working on his boat, and when I got there, he emerged from the cabin looking unkempt. He said, "Hi." I said, "Bye."

I received four phone calls from Frank, none of which earned him a date. But he continued to pursue me.

When I told him my friend Alberta was visiting from Philadelphia, Frank said I could bring her along on a date because we were only going to the Barnegat lighthouse by boat.

As could be expected, Frank's appearance had improved—and soon after, we realized we were meant for each other.

I learned a valuable life lesson that I've carried with me ever since: Don't make snap judgments concerning a person. I almost missed a blessed 45-year marriage to a truly wonderful man.

—*Florence Clay, Fort Myers, Florida*

MATCHED BY DADS. Newlyweds Florence and Frank Clay began dating thanks to their fathers George Emond (far left) and John Clay (far right).

The only rock I know that stays steady, the only institution I know that works, is the family.

—Lee Iacocca

Love & World War II

A TEENAGE SWEETHEART WHO BECAME A SOLDIER REMAINED CLOSE AT HEART.

By Margie Sheek, Clinton, Missouri

I vividly recall waiting for Morris Sheek on July 4, 1944. A young farm girl in Missouri, I watched the lane leading to our home for a Model A Ford coupe driven by a handsome boy who'd asked me to go with him to the neighborhood Fourth of July party.

We'd gotten to know each other through the local Baptist church our families attended. But this was our first date, and I could feel the excitement growing with every beat of my heart.

Little did Morris and I know what the future, in those turbulent times, held in store for us.

Morris was about to start his senior year of high school, and I was several years behind him, the youngest in a family of 10. My parents were protective, and the fact that they'd permitted me to attend this party was a miracle.

Our relationship grew, and for three months, we dated once each week. Morris was on the basketball team and I was a cheerleader, so we saw each other through school activities, too.

In late October, Morris boarded our school bus with an official-looking envelope in his hand. He showed the letter to the other boys, and their excited voices spread the news quickly.

"Greetings, you have been selected…" Morris read. It was his invitation to Uncle Sam's service.

Only two short weeks later, Morris and I had to say goodbye as he headed off for basic training in Louisiana.

After 12 weeks of training, Morris received a seven-day furlough and came home to spend time with his family and friends before shipping out. We made a commitment to wait for each other until he returned from the war.

Waiting for Word

In March 1945, Morris sailed from New York to Germany, where World War II was dragging on. He left before he could take part in his high school graduation ceremony, and his mother attended to accept his diploma for him.

As I had the previous summer, I found myself watching our lane. Only

REUNITED. Morris Sheek (shown below as a young GI) and his childhood sweetheart, Margie Dalton, were married in 1947 (left).

this time, I was waiting for the postman to deliver letters or photographs from Morris.

Poring over every letter he wrote, I learned that he did his share of digging foxholes and eating Army rations. After receiving a promotion, he trained for the military police. Then he was issued a motorcycle and had to check the papers of anyone trying to cross the German border.

In winter of 1945, Morris and three other soldiers were sent to capture a Nazi official hiding in the mountains. They approached the hideaway with guns drawn, ordering him out. Much to their surprise, he quietly emerged and surrendered.

In late summer of 1946, Morris received an honorable discharge. Together with other hometown boys, he made his way back to Clinton, Missouri.

Family and friends were waiting to embrace the returning heroes. When Morris arrived, I was there as his faithful sweetheart, who had been true to her commitment to wait for him.

I was about to start my last year of high school, and we honored our promise to my father to set a wedding date after my graduation.

We've now been married for 64 years and have five children, as well as many grandchildren and great-grandchildren. We've remained a happy couple through the good times and bad, and we thank God for bringing us together.

new neighbors spiced up our lives

A LIVELY JEWISH FAMILY OFFERED A PROTESTANT ONE FRIENDSHIP, FOOD AND FREQUENT HIGH JINKS.

By Eunice Jensen, Anoka, Minnesota

So much joy came into our lives when the Haskvitz family moved in next door to us in Anoka, Minnesota, in the 1940s.

It created a wondrous mix of personalities, religions and ethnic traditions. They were a Jewish family; we were second-generation Swedish-American Protestants.

My mother, Eleanor Anderson, and Rose Haskvitz soon became the best of friends and were each other's comfort and joy in those difficult financial times. By nature, my mother was not prone to any monkey business, but when Rose came on the scene, things changed in a hurry.

I can still hear Rose's musical voice give a happy sort of reprimand/command: "Oh, El, don't be such a stick-in-the-mud. Who needs to have such a clean house anyway? Come on, kids, get in the car."

Mother would drop her dust cloth, and off we'd go, singing all the way to Minneapolis as Rose drove the old Ford with relaxed abandon. I could feel our Swedish reserve blowing right out the car windows.

Living Adventurously

On one occasion, the accelerator pedal to the car was broken, but Mother and Rose didn't let that little problem deter them. My mother knelt down on the floor in front and held the pedal in place so they could chug their way to the grocery store.

I didn't know any other mothers in the 1940s who would put on their husbands' work coveralls and big jackets to join their kids on the toboggan slope. Even though they destroyed our beautifully banked turns, we couldn't stop laughing as they bounced, squealing with glee, all the way down the hill, coming to an abrupt halt when they hit the back steps of the house. We had crazy mothers, and we loved it!

Once, when Mother and Dad were on an errand and my sister and I were minding a chicken roasting in the oven, Rose arrived in a panic. "Where's El? What's she making for supper?" After our answer, Rose wrote this note: "I've taken your kids and your chicken. If you want supper, come to our house. Rose."

Rose had unexpected company coming, and with the food she had in her house plus our chicken, there would be enough for everyone. Spontaneity had come into our lives.

> *I've taken your kids and your chicken. If you want supper, come to our house.*

GARLIC, RDA-GID

Holiday to Remember

One Christmas, after supper, we were part of "talent time" at the Haskvitz home. Everyone had to sing a song, dance, tell a joke, do a magic trick, read a poem or just make some funny faces. Anything was acceptable, and everyone received applause and cheers.

Our family had experienced nothing like that in our lives, and we hadn't suspected or dared to consider that we might have talents. It was fun and freeing, and Rose got us into the mood when she sat down at the old upright piano and played, by ear, any song if we'd all sing together.

The happy bunch was singing Christmas carols until Grandpa Max, Rose's father, said, "Stop the music! What's going on here? 'Joy to the world, the Lord is come'...this is Jewish music? Oy vey!" Then everyone burst out laughing. Grandpa Max taught us some Jewish songs and how to dance the hora.

Our Swedish-American family was introduced to matzo ball soup, corned beef, pastrami, chopped chicken liver, latkes, bagels and lox, and other Jewish dishes we'd never tasted before. But the real gastronomic zest added to our lives was garlic.

Garlic was not a staple in our family, but suddenly Mother's recipes called for putting a little garlic in the soup, the pot roast and the dressing, plus rubbing it on roast chicken. If something was good, garlic made it better.

Thus, our lives were made much more delicious in countless ways by the wonderful family that moved into the house next door... and into our hearts as well.

FIRST COMMUNION DAY. "My brother's first communion in 1965 was a family event," says Robert Gouveia of Burlington, Massachusetts. "In the photo, Stevie is wearing a white suit and posing with family members at our home in Burlington." Shown in the back row are (from left) Robert's aunt, Lena Marashio; her daughters Maryann Gelormini and Nancy Marashio (holding Maryann's son Billy); Robert's mother, Mary Gouveia; and Steve's godfather, Manuel Paul.

Family Portraits

TIMELY TRADITION. Daisy Christie of West Covina, California, shares this 1943 photo of her family in New York. She explains that on Mother's Day at that time, it was customary to wear a red flower if your mother was living or a white one if she had passed away. Daisy (second from left) and her siblings, James, Dorothy and Robert Jr., wore white because their mother had died some years before. Her father, Robert (center), wore a red flower, as his mother was still living.

ANOTHER ERA. "I cherish this photo of my family, taken around 1911 in Yakima, Washington," says Alice Schindler from Bremerton, Washington. "Shown with me, the little girl in the white dress, are my parents, Clarence and Carrie Shupe, my brother Burton and my sister Lois."

learning together

Pictured in this slide from 1959 are my father, Henry Anderson, and me at our home in Westfield, New Jersey. I was 7 years old and a member of the Indian Guides club. We learned a lot about American Indian history, customs and traditions from interested fathers, including mine.

—*Don Anderson, Santaquin, Utah*

CHAPTER 7

That's
ENTERTAINMENT

page 160

From star-studded Hollywood movies and professional sports to TV and radio shows, fun pastimes and events have long been abundant in the United States.

"One day in 1939, we got up at the crack of dawn to take the 'A' trolley to the end of the line," says John Hirsh of Fort Lauderdale, Florida. "We caught the subway downtown, then walked to the Paramount theater, arriving before 10 a.m. to get a ticket for 25 cents. I don't remember the movie—it wasn't why we'd made the trip. We were there to see Tommy Dorsey and his orchestra.

"Tommy Dorsey had a number of hit songs during the 1930s, when swing music was popular, and it was so exciting to see a show in person. I'll never forget watching the orchestra rise from the pit playing their theme song, *I'm Getting Sentimental Over You*.

"They also played *Song of India*. Later, when I joined the service, I found out that this song was vastly more romantic than the real place! But I always had great memories of seeing a thrilling performance."

Yes, spectacular entertainment is one of the delights of life in America.

page 156

page 161

All Shook Up

FOR AN INSTANT, ELVIS' STAR POWER MADE A YOUNG MOM SWOON.

By Joan Ellis, Daytona Beach, Florida

I was a 22-year-old mother of two boys in 1956 when I heard the news: Elvis Presley was coming to Daytona Beach! My 15-year-old sister, Susan, her friend Sandy, my mother and I were beside ourselves with excitement, and we quickly got tickets to see Elvis.

My husband, John, was stationed at Sanford Naval Air Station, close enough for me to drive over to Daytona Beach and catch the show at Peabody Auditorium.

Everyone knew of Elvis. He had appeared on Ed Sullivan's TV show and had shaken, rattled and rolled his way to stardom.

And to think, he was coming to our town. It was just too much!

The day of the concert, Susan and Sandy skipped school and rode up and down Atlantic Avenue, the motel strip along the beach in Daytona, searching for Elvis' pink Cadillac with white-walled tires. They spotted it at the Copacabana Motel on Silver Beach Boulevard.

When they phoned us with the news, Mom, my two little boys and I hurried over to the Copacabana.

And suddenly, there he was—tall, dark and incredibly handsome. Elvis wore black slacks and a shirt with rolled-up sleeves that was tied at the waist, and he paused to exchange pleasantries and pose for pictures with fans. He was very unassuming and extremely polite.

As Elvis put his arms around me for our picture, he said, "I'm having a party after the show, if you'd like to come."

Would I!

My heart skipped a beat until I remembered my two young boys—Steve, age 2, and Scott, a babe in arms—and my hubby back at the base. My sister was furious with me for declining Elvis' invitation.

Leaving my boys with Papa, I joined Susan, Sandy and Mom for the show. We sat in the second row, with Mom on the aisle. Mom got so caught up in the excitement of it all that she slid right off her seat! We never let her forget it and have had many a good laugh remembering it.

After taking Mom home following the performance, Susan and I drove back around to the stage door and saw Elvis smooching with one of his adoring fans.

Curiously, my husband neither made any comment nor showed any jealousy while I shared my adventure of that evening.

But 35 years later, one of John's former Navy buddies, with whom we were reminiscing, told me my husband was so jealous at the time that "he wanted to go punch Elvis out."

This not only made me smile, but also thankful for not giving in to temptation and attending the post-show party!

a turtle from tom mix

SHELLING OUT A DIME AND BOX TOPS BROUGHT A LINK TO A 1930s COWBOY HERO.

By Tom Harvill, Forest City, North Carolina

It wasn't just your run-of-the-mill turtle sitting on a rock or crawling alongside the road. No way. It was a real, genuine, honest-to-goodness Tom Mix turtle.

I know, because right there on the shell was printed "TM."

Who's Tom Mix?

Well, if you're old enough to remember a 7-year-old Shirley Temple and the Little Rascals when they were called "Our Gang" and listened to *Gang Busters*, you probably recall Tom Mix.

Back in the mid-1930s, there were no TVs. Kids went to Saturday matinees at the picture show and followed serials on the radio.

When you listened to *Little Orphan Annie*, *Renfrew of the Mounted* and *Jack Armstrong, the All-American Boy*, you discovered that you could send for all kinds of gadgets, code rings and secret whistles that made your favorite radio heroes come alive.

The same was true for youngsters like me who were fans of *The Tom Mix Ralston Straight Shooters* radio show. I saved Ralston cereal box tops until I had enough, then sent the box tops along with a dime or so in order to get the turtle that was advertised.

The little oblong box containing a turtle took 2 or 3 weeks to get to me through the mail. Was I excited when it finally arrived!

Believe it or not, that little fellow was alive after several days of being jostled and bounced around while cooped up in that tiny box. The only thing that saved him, as far as I could tell, was his size.

He was about the diameter of a silver dollar, and right there on the dark brown shell was "TM" as plain as can be.

I kept my new pet turtle in a shallow pan of water and put a flat rock in the center for him to sit on. I don't remember what I fed that little guy. Lettuce, maybe.

From Movie Reels to Radio

Tom Mix was a silent-screen cowboy, preceding legends such as Ken Maynard and John Wayne. Tom was one of Hollywood's biggest silent-screen stars. He lived high, spent money as he made it and lost millions of dollars in the stock market crash of 1929.

STAR QUALITY. Tom Mix is pictured at left in a publicity shot from his 1932 film *Destry Rides Again*. The popular cowboy showman starred in many Westerns, mostly during the silent movie era, and was one of the author's boyhood favorites.

When the talkies came in, Tom went out. He joined a circus for a while, and in 1933, the Ralston Purina Company agreed to sponsor a 15-minute radio show. It wasn't really Tom on the show—he was impersonated by an actor—but it was still a huge success with kids like me.

Tom seemed the epitome of the Western cowboy. After seeing Buffalo Bill's Wild West show, he decided he wanted to be a showman.

As a younger man, Tom joined the Army when the United States got involved in the Spanish-American War in 1898. He became a sergeant but never saw action.

A few years before his death in 1940 in an automobile accident, my mom took my brother and me to see a Tom Mix circus when it came to town. It was such a thrill.

Tom did rope tricks, stunt riding on his horse, Tony, and even some fancy shooting. Before we went home, Mom bought us each a genuine Tom Mix whip—a leather thong on a

COWBOY WANNA-BE. The author, shown at far right with his father and brother Jack in Walnut, California, was a big fan of *The Tom Mix Ralston Straight Shooters* radio show of the 1930s and also went to a Tom Mix circus.

bamboo stick that popped in a very satisfying way whenever we snapped it.

After all these years, I don't recall what happened to my prized pet. I do remember watching him swim around in his pan, crawl up on his rock and stick out his long neck, as if to say "Howdy."

And I'll always remember how exciting it was for a young kid to receive a real, genuine, honest-to-goodness Tom Mix turtle.

WESTERN BEST

As a girl growing up on the farm, I loved stories of the Wild West and idolized the cowboy stars of the late 1940s. Roy Rogers, Gene Autry and the Lone Ranger were some of my favorites.

On Saturday afternoons, when our family went to Minot, North Dakota, for our weekly shopping trips, my sister Shirley and I would attend the weekly Westerns at the Orpheum Theater for 12 cents a ticket. My heroes always prevailed over dishonest villains.

I would spend part of my weekly allowance on comic books about my heroes, and I read them as often as I could.

In 1949, I entered a Roy Rogers contest and was thrilled to receive a postcard from Roy and Dale Evans, which I have kept and treasured all these years.

The cowboy heroes of the 1940s and '50s gave young people someone to look up to. They were role models who taught us about courage and honesty and helped us become responsible adults.

—*Ardella Score, Minot, North Dakota*

I Never Dreamed I'd Become a
Rockette!

TAP LESSONS LED TO A CAREER AMONG RADIO CITY MUSIC HALL'S HIGH-KICKING DANCERS.

By Rita Macjeski Monsees, Garden City, New York

Dancing has been a gift in my life, and I performed with many organizations over the years. But I never imagined that one day I'd become a Rockette at Radio City Music Hall in New York City.

In the summer of 1942, I was studying tap dancing in a New York studio when the teacher suggested I try out for the Rockettes.

I had no idea what to expect and was very nervous. I auditioned using the dance routine my instructor had taught me, plus was asked to perform kicks.

Imagine how excited I was to receive

an invitation to attend a rehearsal for the new show! I met Russell Markert, who had created the Rockettes dance team, and Emily Sherman, captain of the Rockettes, and we practiced a routine.

I was shown the dressing room on the third floor and underwent fittings for my costume.

Many costumes were made with parts from older costumes, and some were quite heavy to wear. I asked if I could keep one when leaving the Rockettes and was told that no one was allowed to keep them. Even the shoes

WHAT A KICK! Although she performed in many venues during her dancing career, the biggest thrill for the author was being a Rockette (top photo). In the photo above, she's fourth from the left in line onstage at New York City's Radio City Music Hall, home of the Rockettes.

were the property of Radio City.

As opening day approached, my knees wouldn't stop shaking, but everything went well and I was now a Rockette. What a thrill!

Of course, it was only for the summer to relieve the permanent girls who were on vacation. But that was fine with me, because I was attending Adelphi College in the fall.

I remember when September came, Russell would say, "Okay, girls, I'll see you next year." This assured us that we were expected back for the next season.

That theater was so impressive. When I took the elevator down to the stage and saw the stage from the wings, it was quite a sight. I remember spotting Ray Bolger, Cary Grant and Lucille Ball watching from the wings.

Footlights Blinded

Once we were on stage, the lights were so bright that we couldn't see the audience. If we got too close to the footlights, as we sometimes did, we could see a row or two.

I was the fourth from the left and always managed to be right near the drummer so I didn't miss a beat.

When we returned to the dressing rooms, Emily, the captain, was there with her notebook to correct any of the girls who had made mistakes in the dances.

It was a very disciplined life, and we rehearsed for the next show while performing the current one. We did four shows a day, 7 days a week, and then we had a week off.

At that time, we performed our routines after the picture, which was usually a first-run movie.

Our dinner hour started about 5 or 6 p.m., and we had a 7 p.m. show. This didn't give us time to remove our makeup, so when we went out, our makeup gave us away as Rockettes. Many times, we barely made it back in time to get into our costumes and get down to the stage.

Once we performed the "doll dance" and had to assemble on the three elevators that were below the stage. I was on the top level as the "doll box"

rose, and we had to stand perfectly still. When the elevator stopped, I was standing several stories above the stage.

We always had a full dress rehearsal—with full makeup and costumes—for each new show at 8 a.m. Many of the girls who traveled from New Jersey, Westchester or Long Island stayed in dormitories overnight.

It was a joyous and interesting life. The girls were all friendly, and we were like one big family. Sometimes my mom and dad invited a few of my friends home after the show to stay overnight. We all had a great time.

When Howard, my future husband, was home on a furlough, he would see the show and meet me at the stage door every night. Then we'd go out to eat before he took me home.

When I got married in 1945, I remained with the Rockettes until I received a teaching offer. In 1946, I was in the lineup for the Easter performances, but I left in 1947 to start teaching elementary school. With the war over, many other girls were choosing to leave the hectic theater life to start families.

I stayed in touch with many of the dancers and others by joining the Rockette alumni club. It was a wonderful time of my life I'll never forget.

Shirley Temple Made Permanent Memories

THOSE MOVIE-STAR CURLS GAVE ONE STRAIGHT-HAIRED GIRL A WHOLE LOT TO THINK BACK ON.

By Marilyn Jensen, La Habra, California

CURLY-CUTE. The author (above) and girls all across the country emulated the hairstyle of Shirley Temple (left).

I was in second grade during the '30s when Shirley Temple danced and dimpled her way across America's silver screens.

Her golden curls (52 of them, according to fan magazines) tumbled adorably from her little head and captured a country's heart.

Mothers everywhere—mine included—took up the challenge of transforming their own offspring into reasonable facsimiles of Shirley.

Before every birthday party or piano recital, I'd be herded into the kitchen, where Mother had the curling iron heating on the stove. She'd lick her finger and touch it to the iron. A sizzling sound indicated it was ready.

"For heaven's sake, stand still," she'd say, brandishing the iron and waving away the first whiff of singed hair.

The result of her efforts was nothing short of a miracle. My well-cowlicked mane was still straight as ever, but I was certain the frizzled border around my ears admitted me to some magic kingdom where only curly-haired movie stars belonged.

Those styling sessions around the stove finally ended when a retired beautician moved into our neighborhood. She agreed to give me a professional permanent in exchange for Mother's making her a dress from some silk she had from China.

Visions of Shirley danced in my head! On

the appointed day I was awake before dawn, eager to meet the beautician.

Hair Nightmare

Alas, I hadn't realized the price I'd pay for curls that would "outlast a party." Acrid fumes from the permanent lotion brought tears to my eyes, and if I wiggled, I got rapped on the head with a comb!

When each strand of hair was tightly wound and secured, I was clamped to a machine that pulled at my hair and sent heat surging through to my scalp.

Exactly how long I was trapped there I don't recall. All I know is that I'd gone to the beautician's right after breakfast, and it was nearly dinnertime before I arrived back home to present myself in all my frizzy glory.

No sweet dumpling curls like Shirley's covered my head, but the machine's results were indeed permanent. I know, because the moment I got home, I stuck my head under the faucet as a test.

The frizz remained, but the set was gone before Mother ever saw it. "I spent all that time sewing that silk dress for you to look like this?" Mother shrieked when she caught sight of my not-so-Shirley-like hair.

Not long ago, I came across an article by some Hollywood insider claiming that Shirley's curls weren't really hers at all—that she simply wore a wig.

Say it ain't so! I'd hate to think that so many of us young girls went through so much to look like something that never was!

STAR STRUCK

There was quite a bit of excitement in our town of New Haven, Connecticut, when Church Street became Hollywood Boulevard for a day.

This photo of Loew's Poli Theatre, 23 Church Street, was taken on August 10, 1939. The Rogers Studio, which had an office in the Poli Building, produced the photograph.

The people lined up on both sides of the theater entrance were waiting to see Mickey Rooney and Judy Garland in person on the stage of the 3,200-seat theater.

The only person I can identify in the picture is Mr. Jacobs. He's the bald man standing in the entrance of his cigar and candy store, immediately to the right of the theater entrance. I don't know when he started his store, but he ran it until just before the theater was torn down, in 1959, to make way for a parking lot.

The little establishment with the white front, just to the left of the theater entrance, was Charles' Lunch, which featured hamburgers. It was commonly known as Nickel Charlie's, although by the time I was a teen, in the late 1950s, the hamburgers were 15 cents each. You could still get coffee for a nickel.

For a good meal, especially the soup, there was the Palace Grill, next to Mr. Jacobs' store. The only problem was that a cup of coffee there was a dime. My solution was a meal at the Palace and coffee at Charles' Lunch.
—*Max Brunswick, New Haven, Connecticut*

Off to the FAIR

GREAT PLATES. "This huge license plate was the hub of the 1964 New York World's Fair," recalls Owen Carpenter of Tucson, Arizona. "I took a photo of my wife, Marion, peeking through the 'P' and our son David in the 'J' of the exhibit."

YEE-HAW! Fifty-two feet tall and billed as the world's tallest cowboy, "Big Tex" greeted visitors at the 1959 Texas State Fair. "This post card is a reflection of the fair I saw while growing up," says Danny Atchley of Mineral Wells, Texas.

People rarely succeed unless they have fun in what they are doing.

—Dale Carnegie

Frankie's Warm-Up Singer

In 1945, Frank Sinatra was a craze. Young and talented, he sang for audiences everywhere. One place he performed was the Paramount Theatre in New York City.

At the time, I was a singer with the Nick Kenny Radio Gang, and I also sang for the men and women in the service at different USO clubs and the American Theatre Wing.

Between shows at the Paramount, Frank would take a limousine to the Park Avenue USO to sing for the boys. I was the singer who kept the huge audience entertained until Frank got there. Wearing beautiful gowns, I did the familiar act of asking a sailor or soldier up to the stage and singing to him, with a big kiss capping it off.

My repertoire of songs included *The Man I Love* and *Stormy Weather*. As Latin music was so popular in the 1940s, I'd sing *Perfidia*, first in English and then in Spanish.

Then came the big announcement: "Ladies and gentlemen, sailors and soldiers, may we present Frank Sinatra!" He'd arrive, and I'd step backstage and swoon. Oh, Frankie!

—*Dorothy Scott, Reseda, California*

Extras in *BEN-HUR*

IN 1925, TWO YOUNG BROTHERS WERE PART OF A LANCE-WIELDING ARMY IN THIS SILENT-MOVIE SPECTACULAR.

By Milton Beyer, Chevy Chase, Maryland

Our family lived in Hollywood in 1925 in a small bungalow at the bottom of a hill in the San Gabriel Canyon. Antonio Moreno, a silent film star at the time, lived in a large house at the top of the hill.

It was a good year for silent films. Charlie Chaplin charmed audiences in *The Gold Rush*, Sergei Eisenstein made *Potemkin* and MGM made *Ben-Hur*, directed by Fred Niblo.

My aunt Esther had a Russian friend who was an assistant director at MGM. They came from the same town near Kiev, and when he had calls for children as extras, he called Aunt Esther. Her two sons got to appear in films with stars such as Douglas Fairbanks, Mary Pickford and Harold Lloyd.

When MGM made *Ben-Hur*, there was a call for a large number of boys and men. This time, my older brother, Joe, and I got to go. Joe was 10 and I was 8.

On the big day, my mother, brother and I caught a trolley car before 7 a.m. and rode to Culver City and the MGM studio. There we joined more than 150 men and boys of all sizes in a large tent, where they had bedouin costumes and makeup artists.

I was dressed in a flowing robe and turban, made up with greasepaint and makeup and given a lance with a pennant attached.

Papier-Mache Mountains

The crowd of extras was assembled in a valley between two papier-mache mountains supported by two-by-fours on the back side. We were the army recruited to rescue Jesus. Arranged according to height, the men were standing in the front, facing the camera and wind machines, with everyone else behind in order of diminishing size.

Some small dolls were stuck in the sand and on the sides of the papier-mache mountains. This was to complete the illusion of a vast horde gathered to liberate Jesus from Pontius Pilate.

After we rehearsed raising our lances and shouting for about two hours, the wind machines were turned on, the cameras started rolling and shooting began.

At the noon break, we each got a box lunch with two white bread sandwiches, a hard-boiled egg, a pickle, fruit, cookies and milk. It was a grand treat.

After lunch, an attempt was made to give the school-age children an educational class, as was required by California law.

By 5 p.m., it was all over. We were back on the trolley and headed home.

There was a bit of added excitement when Mom discovered she had left our pay envelopes, containing $7 each, in her purse on the trolley. She told a nearby police officer about it. The officer chased down the trolley and returned with her purse.

Waited Three Years to See It

I finally saw the film in 1928 with my father and brother at the Hill Street Theater in Los Angeles. I remember that because it was the same day Charles Lindbergh came to town on the nationwide tour that followed his flight across the Atlantic the year before. We went to the movie instead of Lindbergh's parade.

In 1985, my wife and I went to see a newly restored print of *Ben-Hur* at the American Film Institute in Washington, D.C. It featured a new musical score, and some of the original two-color Technicolor scenes were added.

When my scene appeared on screen, uncut and restored, I couldn't restrain myself. I jumped up, shouting, "That's my scene! That's my scene!"

let's go to DISNEY

BACK IN THE FUTURE. Bruce Perkins and Cassie Fraley got a chance to chat with space travelers in 1961 while visiting Disneyland with Cassie's parents, Bob and Ruth Fraley, of Show Low, Arizona.

Laughter is America's most important export.

—Walt Disney

AND MICKEY, TOO. "I was going through some old papers and found this menu from a trip I took to Disneyland in 1955, the year it first opened," says Sharlene Gill of Fort Wayne, Indiana. "I was 18 and was impressed by this new theme-park concept. The prices for menu items were pretty unbelievable, too. Oh, those were the good old days!"

Carnation in Disneyland

SANDWICHES

Cheeseburger	55c	Hamburger	45c

With Lettuce, Tomato, Pickle and Relish.

American Cheese (Grilled or Plain)	30c
Ham (Grilled or Plain)	50c
Ham and Cheese (Grilled or Plain)	60c
Tuna Salad	40c
Hot Dog (Premium Frank with Tasty Pickle Relish)	25c

All Sandwiches Delightfully Garnished with Dairy Fresh Carnation Cottage Cheese.

SALADS

Cottage Cheese with Choice of Pineapple, Pears or Peaches	65c
Fruit Bowl with Sherbet, Banana and Whipped Cream	65c
Crisp Green Salad	65c

SPECIALITIES

Soup of the Day	25c
Chili and Beans	40c
Cheeseburger Size	70c

PIES and CAKES

Pie	20c	Pie a la Mode	35c
Cake	20c	Cake a la Mode	35c

BEVERAGES

Milk (half-pint)	10c
Buttermilk (half-pint)	10c
Chocolate Drink (half-pint)	10c
Coffee	10c
Tea (Iced or Hot)	10c
Coca Cola	10c
Pepsi Cola	10c
Sarsaparilla	10c
Phosphate (Cherry or Lemon)	10c
Root Beer	10c
Welch's Grape Juice	15c

FEATURES FROM FRONTIERLAND

Golden West Float	30c

An invigorating Orange Freeze.

Log Cabin Sundae	40c

A tasty Caramel Sundae topped with a miniature log cabin of pretzel sticks.

Sante Fe Express	60c

Miniature choo-choo, 5 scoops of ice cream; strawberries, pineapple, chocolate; banana wheels, marshmallow, whipped cream and cherry.

Old Timer	40c

An old-fashioned treat made with Peppermint Stick Ice Cream, strawberries, pineapple, whipped cream and cherry.

TREATS FROM Fantasyland

Castle Special	70c

Castle with 5 scoops of ice cream, marshmallow topping, 2 whole bananas.

Snow White Sundae	35c

Marshmallow sundae topped with grated coconut.

Mad Hatter Sundae	25c

Small chocolate sundae garnished with salted peanuts.

Carnation in Disneyland Special	79c

One of the world's largest sundaes. 5 scoops of ice cream, sliced pineapple, 5 different sundae toppings, sliced banana, chopped almonds, whipped cream and cherry.

Peter Pan Sundae	45c

5 scoops of chocolate ice cream, marshmallow topping, chopped almonds, whipped cream and cherry.

SURPRISES FROM TOMORROWLAND

T. W. A. Rocket Ship Special	75c

Space Ship ready to blast off, 4 scoops of ice cream an ice cream cone, cherry and marshmallow toppings, and banana.

2000 A.D. Special	79c

We predict that health foods will never replace this tasty treat . . . a delicious hot fudge sundae.

Inter-Planet Special	45c

2 scoops vanilla ice cream, topped with fruit salad, whipped cream and cherry.

Martian Sundae	45c

2 scoops of vanilla ice cream, hot caramel topping, sprinkling of malted milk powder, sliced peaches, whipped cream and cherry.

IMPORTS FROM Adventureland

Hawaiian Sundae	50c

Vanilla and strawberry ice cream with pineapple, strawberries, coconut, sliced banana and sliced pineapple.

Amazon Special	55c

Hot fudge over 2 large scoops of vanilla ice cream, banana, chopped almonds, whipped cream and cherry.

Tropical Sundae	55c

Tasty treat made with 2 scoops of ice cream, quartered banana, pineapple topping, whipped cream and cherry.

Tahitian Sundae	40c

2 scoops of vanilla ice cream, with chocolate topping and salted peanuts.

SUGGESTIONS FROM MAIN STREET

Old Mill Strawberry Sundae	35c

Two scoops of Vanilla Ice Cream, covered with fresh frozen strawberries, whipped cream and cherry.

Victorian Banana Split	55c

Vanilla, chocolate, strawberry ice cream, topped with strawberries, pineapple, banana, chopped almonds, whipped cream and cherry.

Gay Nineties Sundaes	35c

Chocolate, Caramel, Cherry, Pineapple, Marshmallow.

Junior Sundaes	25c
Old Fashioned Ice Cream Sodas	30c

Vanilla, Pineapple, Lemon, Chocolate, Root Beer, Coffee, Strawberry, Cherry.

Town Square Malted Milks or Shakes	35c

Vanilla Pineapple, Coffee, Chocolate, Root Beer, Strawberry and Cherry.

Gibson Girl Parfait	45c

3 scoops of ice cream with fresh frozen strawberries, almonds, whipped cream and cherry.

Almond-Marshmallow Sundae	40c

2 scoops of chocolate ice cream, with marshmallow, chopped almonds, whipped cream and cherry.

Cinnamon Sundae	40c

Vanilla and strawberry ice cream, strawberry and pineapple topping, chopped almonds, whipped cream and cherry.

Lover's Delight	45c

Strawberry and vanilla ice cream, marshmallow and strawberry topping, chopped almonds, whipped cream and cherry.

Hot Caramel Sundae	45c

2 large scoops of vanilla ice cream, with hot caramel, chopped almonds, whipped cream and cherry.

Black and White Sundae	45c

Chocolate and vanilla ice cream with marshmallow and chocolate, chopped almonds, whipped cream and cherry.

Tandem Dish of Ice Cream	25c

(Please Do Not Ask For Substitutions!)

We Feature Swift's Premium Meats, Maxwell House Coffee, Van Camp Tuna

FLOOR SEATING. "You rarely see a television like the one in this photo anymore," says Norma Jean Hissong of Olympia, Washington. "My siblings and I were sprawled all over the floor with our father, Norman Stafford, watching 1955's version of a big-screen TV. Judy is the blonde closest to the television, and the rest of us are (from left) Artie, Ronnie, me and Dobbie. That's an aquarium sitting on top of the TV. One day, Ronnie was swinging a cane around and hit the aquarium. We had water everywhere!"

TV TIME!

CALLING ON UNCLE MILTIE

My best friend's family got the first TV in our neighborhood. It was the mid-1940s, and everyone envied them.

When Milton Berle—"Uncle Miltie"—was "Mr. Television" and appeared on Tuesday nights with *Texaco Star Theater,* I developed a routine. I'd go down to my friend's house every Tuesday about 8 o'clock and ask, "Can Billy come out and play?"

They always invited me in. I'd stay until Uncle Miltie was done, and then I'd go home.

I don't think they caught on until one evening when I showed up in the pouring rain and asked, "Can Billy come out and play?"

—*John Hutchinson, Dorchester, New Jersey*

EARLY HOME THEATER

The few televisions that were around in 1948 were tiny and difficult to watch. However, our aunt Amy's had a 21-inch screen, which was huge for the time.

The TV was set into the wall above a mantelpiece at one end of her long living room, which became the viewing area. With two low built-in bookcases on either side of the entrance, the area seemed like a theater. Folding chairs scattered around for extra viewers added to the impression.

Each Sunday evening, a number of her friends would gather to watch *Toast of the Town*, Ed Sullivan's variety show. In another part of the room, my sister and I would chat quietly with our aunt.

She always saw to it that everyone had refreshments. When the show was over and the lights came on, guests would thank my aunt and head to their cars. A few traveled as far as 10 miles to her comfortable home in southeastern Pennsylvania.

In later years, a sister lived in the house. With a picture, she covered the place where the TV was once the center of attention.

—*Mary Beale Wright, New Port Richey, Florida*

WE ALL LOVED LUCY

In the early 1950s, when our family went to town to do our shopping, we always stopped at my brother-in-law's house to watch programs for a while on their Admiral TV set.

Our favorite shows were Sid Caesar's *Your Show of Shows* and *I Love Lucy*. One night, my wife, Christine, was sitting in a platform rocker while we watched.

Lucy's show was even funnier than usual that night; we were all enjoying it immensely. But Christine laughed so hard that she turned the rocker over backward, dumping herself onto the floor.

When she kept laughing as she lay there, we knew she wasn't hurt. But we've never let her forget the night she really loved Lucy!

—*Donald Catt, Flat Rock, Illinois*

brush with
THE BABE

TREASURE AWAITED A YOUNG FAN IN "THE HOUSE THAT RUTH BUILT."

By Robert Layton, Mechanicsville, Virginia

It was June of 1948, and for me (at left), excitement filled the air in our New Jersey town of West Belmar.

I'd soon turn 12, and my birthday was to include a trip to Yankee Stadium in New York City with my dad to see the "Bronx Bombers."

A major-league baseball game was, and remains, a big treat for a boy not yet a teenager. And there was a bonus—a two-inning exhibition by some Yankees old-timers as part of the famous ballpark's 25th anniversary celebration.

My heartbeat quickened outside the stadium when I, along with other fans there, received a commemorative photograph of the legendary Babe Ruth. The day's festivities were to include a ceremony retiring Ruth's uniform number, old No. 3.

The old-timers' game concluded with a roar of approval for the stars of yesteryear.

From my seat in the mezzanine, I could see "The Great One" seated right behind the Yankees dugout. I thought, *What if I could talk to the Bambino?*

I asked my dad, "Do you think Mr. Ruth would sign my picture?"

"I doubt you could get close to him," was Dad's seasoned reply.

A Boy Determined

"Can I at least try?" I asked. No sooner had my compassionate father replied, "Why not?" than I was off.

I was only a few steps down the aisle of the section where Ruth sat when a guard had me in his grasp. With the determination of a racehorse headed for the finish line, I broke free and continued to advance.

I got close before being corralled by another guard. Ruth, sitting with his nurse, noticed the commotion and came to my aid. "It's OK, it's a picture," the Babe said. His raspy voice had been weakened by throat cancer.

Trembling, I passed the photograph to the famous home-run hitter. Pay dirt! And then I realized I had no pen.

Looking up the aisle, I saw the struggling arms and legs of another young fan with the same goal. He was holding a photo and a pen.

I snapped up the pen and print from the boy and returned to Ruth. Shakily, I handed him the pen and both photos, which he signed. After thanking him, I returned the pen and one photo to the other boy.

My father's pride equaled my own, as he had witnessed the whole episode from above. On the subway home, however, I was confronted with a tough decision about my signed photo (at left).

An older boy offered me his three-ring binder of autographs in exchange for my new Ruth treasure. Names like Tommy Henrich, Phil Rizzuto, Bill Dickey, Joe DiMaggio and Yogi Berra jumped off the binder's pages.

"What should I do?" I asked my dad.

"That's a decision only you can make," he said.

I deliberated long and hard, examining the notebook, then turning to the signed photo. In the end, I walked away, pleased with my choice.

Babe Ruth was to live only about two months more after the day he signed my photo. It was his final appearance at Yankee Stadium and the last time he wore his famous No. 3.

I looked at that photo almost every day for more than 50 years while it hung in my office at home. I have since given the treasure to my son.

I am comforted knowing that this cherished possession remains with someone who will always appreciate the joy it has given me.

FORBES FIELD in Pittsburgh was the scene as the Pirates hosted a game in 1949. "That was the year the Pirates' Ralph Kiner hit 54 homers," recalls Richard Haywood of Laurel, Maryland, whose father, Gerald, took this slide. "My Little League team usually attended a major league game twice a year."

here she comes...

ROYAL COURT. "I was a princess (right) for the 1948 Tournament of Roses Parade in Pasadena, California," says Dorothy Young Osborn, who lives in San Diego. She is shown on the left front of the float in the photo above.

BLACK STOCKINGS apparently went with anything, even a swimsuit, in the early 1930s. "My sister worked as a waitress in Ocean City, New Jersey, and one of the customers she served bought this postcard and sent it to her," says Doris Hinnegan of Feasterville, Pennsylvania. "It shows Miss St. Louis in the Miss America Pageant's Bathing Revue Parade on the famous boardwalk in Atlantic City."

a face for television

My mother, Louise Wallis Hughes, was 17 when she won a silver loving cup as Miss Television 1928 at the Seventh Annual Chicago Radio Show.

From a total of 19 contestants, judges selected my mother as "the girl whose image and voice are most beautiful when transmitted by television," according to a newspaper article about the event.

The newspaper article also said, "Miss Television had dark-brown hair, a pretty smile and a clear, pleasing voice. Television acting, experts said, will be the entertainment of the future. And 'Miss Television,' they believe, is the type that will prove most popular."

Representing Chicago and Illinois, my mother went on to compete for the title of Queen of American Beauty, a contest sponsored by the National Hairdressers and Cosmetologists Association, at the Masonic Temple in Detroit.

Newspapers at the time routinely called this event the Miss America contest, but it was actually an alternative to the real Miss America pageant, which was not held from 1928 to 1932.

One article noted, "Face, figure and the coiffure of the hair will count a third each. The grand prize will be $100 in gold."

—David Hughes, Grass Valley, California

CHAPTER 8

Small Town, BIG CITY

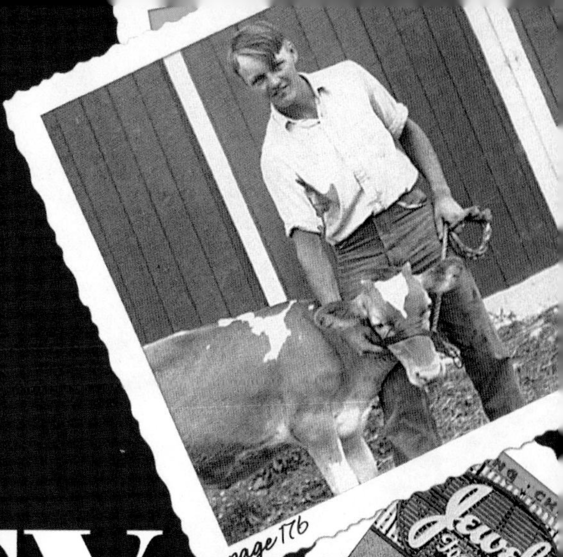
page 176

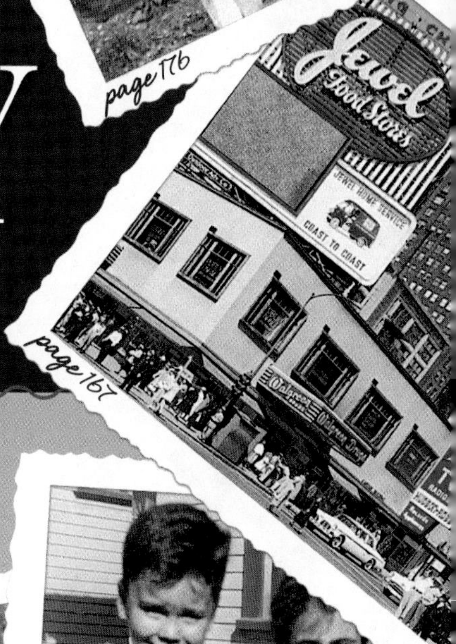
Jewel
Food Stores
page 167

Backyards in these United States range from quiet farm fields to skyscrapers. But whatever locale Americans call home, they have enduring memories of the people and places there.

"I'll never forget the day I was walking with a friend of mine in Hope, Arkansas, during the mid-1930s," says Travis White of Tucson, Arizona. "Gerald and I came upon some men working at Third Street and Main.

"Curious, we stopped and watched them for a while. Suddenly Gerald exclaimed, 'I know what they're doing! They're putting in a traffic light!'

"I asked, 'What's a traffic light?' Gerald explained about stopping on red and going on green. He informed me that cars have to wait at a red light even if there are no other cars around.

"They sure picked the right intersection for that light. It was the busiest intersection in Hope. But it did look kind of funny on Saturdays, when all the farmers came to town and you'd see all those wagons, horses and mules waiting at the light."

Read on to "visit" more American hometowns. Chances are, it will take you back to yours.

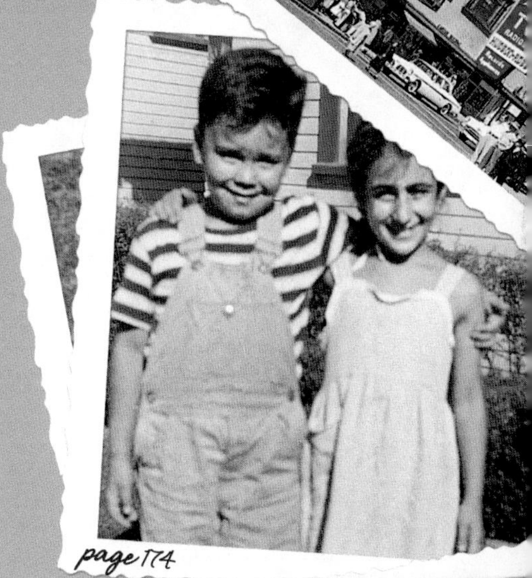
page 174

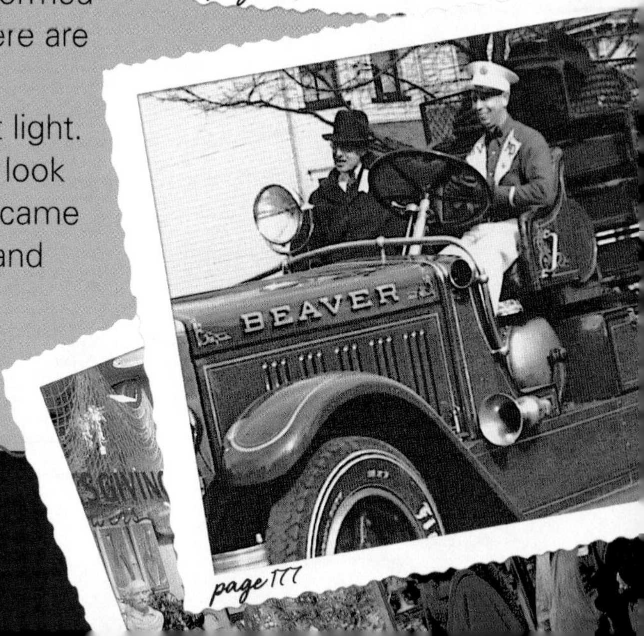
BEAVER
page 177

Like Bedford Falls

MEMORIES OF AN IDYLLIC HOMETOWN CALL TO MIND THE FICTIONAL BUT PICTURE-PERFECT LOCALE IN A HEARTWARMING MOVIE.

By Bradley Shane, North Arlington, New Jersey

The town of Rutherford, New Jersey has become what many people call a "bedroom community," a place to sleep and eat before heading off to jobs in New York City or elsewhere.

But when I was a child, during the 1960s, Rutherford was "Small Town, USA," resembling Bedford Falls from the movie *It's a Wonderful Life*. The main street was Park Avenue, where you could easily envision a horse and carriage rattling over cobblestones or Model T Fords puttering along.

On the west end of town, stores and shops with false-front rooftops of differing heights gave Rutherford the appearance of a Western town. Many a time, I'd ride my bicycle to the hilly streets and look down on the rows of stores, pretending that I was a cowboy heading over a ridge and spying a town where I could rest my horse and wet my whistle.

At Christmastime, strings of large lightbulbs in red, green, blue and white were hung over the avenues from streetlight to streetlight, and I got covered with falling snow as I walked along and shopped at night with my mother. Santa Claus would walk the streets wishing all a merry Christmas while handing out candy canes to the kids.

Mom and I always stopped at LeGrand's, a paint and hardware store that filled its storefront windows with toys like metal military men, rubber farm animals, cars and trucks.

MAE-MOON (bottom), a store for women, had "stores everywhere," according to its sign. Drucker's (below) was "sort of an upscale 5- and 10-cent store," explains the author.

THE RIVOLI THEATRE in Rutherford, New Jersey, is shown above in 1922.

I was always delighted when my mother would ask, "Which ones do you want?"

Window Shopping

My friends and I would also stare into the windows at R&S Auto and Hardware, and we'd admire the new bikes—red ones and green ones, some with baskets and lights or streamers hanging down from the handle grips. R&S also sold extras like horns, mud flaps and mirrors.

I knew Santa shopped there because one or two of those bicycles ended up under our tree! I later worked at the shop, but by then the name had been changed and the magic was gone.

At Werner's—Menswear, it was a pleasure just to look at the finery in the store windows, like men's hats resting atop wooden pedestals, only the finest suits and wool overcoats. I was a Boy Scout, and Werner's was the only place I knew of then that sold Boy Scout supplies.

Next to Werner's was the Rivoli Theatre, where ushers with red vests carried flashlights to show patrons their seats and said "Shhh" to kids who laughed or talked during a movie.

My mom shopped at Mae-Moon, a store selling women's garments. The interesting thing in this shop was the vacuum tube used to send money off to the main office, high above the sales floor. The canister, containing correct change, would return through the tube, flying across the ceiling and down to the cashier.

Our Woolworth, the classic 5- and 10-cent store, still had its glass display cases that had to be opened by a salesgirl with a small brass key. I remember the countertops divided into many wooden sections and holding everything from spools of thread of every conceivable color to cards with buttons stitched to them.

Though 78-rpm records were waning, Woolworth still sold them. I recall flipping through them in the wooden bins, having to read the label in the center to find the song and artist. Only a paper sleeve protected the 78s, unlike the colorful cardboard sleeves of the LPs coming into the store.

On Saturdays, kids would pack the D&D Magic Shop, located in Rutherford's Station

Square. The men who owned the shop were always ready to show us kids a new trick or two. I slowly built up a pretty impressive magic kit and even bought an old, tin-covered suitcase to contain it all.

Memorable Museum

Rutherford also had its own museum on the second floor of an old building. On the way up the creaky steps, you'd pass a stuffed bear that, over time, seemed to have all of its claws pulled out for souvenirs.

The bear's companion was a stuffed wildcat of some kind that reportedly escaped a zoo and was shot by a Rutherford man. I never knew if the story was true or if the beast simply came from someone's attic.

The museum also had a rock and mineral display that inspired me to go chipping away at every rock in our yard and neighborhood in hopes of discovering one with crystals; I never did find any. Our hometown museum may have lacked sophistication, but it was ours!

A coal delivery in town was always a big event. If one of my pals yelled that someone was getting a delivery, bicycles would quickly appear from out of garages or behind homes, and we'd be off to watch.

If the delivery truck could get close enough to the house, the coal men ran a chute from the truck bed to the window of the coal bin. Usually, the strong men had to carry the coal in large baskets on their backs and pour the coal into the chute connected to the window.

What a noise there was as 50 pounds of coal from each basket pounded down the chute! We heard a wonderful hissing sound as the coal hit the floor of the bin.

A coal furnace provided great heat, but it wasn't as simple as turning a dial on the wall. You woke to a cold morning until someone got up and stoked the fire with coal. I'd huddle close to a kerosene lamp on the dining room table while waiting for the furnace to heat the cast-iron radiators.

One of my lasting memories of Rutherford is from Christmastime, when I attended the town's tree lighting with my girlfriend on an unforgettable night.

To some people there, the thick fog that rolled in may have dampened the festive spirit a bit, but to me, it was perfect. There were carriage rides, hot chocolate and caroling.

The unforgettable moment for me came with the clip-clop of horse hooves. Suddenly, out of the fog, there appeared a horse with a black bridle, bells of gold jingling and steam billowing from its breath, looking very much like something out of a movie.

A small town is a place where there's no place to go where you shouldn't.

—Burt Bacharach

sweet home chicago

WATERWORKS. "This photo shows the Olson Rug Company waterfall, which was located at Crawford (Pulaski) and Diversey Avenues in Chicago," recalls Josephine Blau of Schaumburg, Illinois. "My daughter, Mary Jo (shown in 1957), still remembers going there. At night, the beautiful waterfall sparkled under colored lights. Many people enjoyed going to see it."

WINDY CITY. "I know the corner of State and Randolph streets in Chicago very well," relates Richard Hahne from Glenview, Illinois. "I worked in the Public Finance office, which was located over the Walgreen drugstore, shown in this postcard from 1957. In fact, the guy on the right-hand corner, wearing the white shirt and light blue pants, is me!"

catching a wave of nostalgia

LIVING THE SURFING LIFE ALONG MONTEREY BAY WAS A TIME OF GLORIOUS FREEDOM.

By Allen Grasso, Coos Bay, Oregon

It was mostly a secret in the late 1950s and 1960s that our village was a surfing Camelot.

Capitola, California, was set like a jewel in a protective green cove, looking like it had fallen out of time with its Victorian houses lining the embracing cliffs.

After World War II, you could live on a Pacific Coast beach with practically no money. Six of us surfers rented an old Victorian for $15 apiece, and each night the village kids came out of the fog to gather there and talk about what had happened at the beach that day.

It was our turn at life, and we made the most of it. We still feel lucky because there may never be a time like it again.

We surfers lived on the edge of an aquatic wilderness. We were different from the valley kids who spent time in hot bowling alleys or racing cars. We lived a more physical life. Our theme song was *Memphis* by Chuck Berry, and we called ourselves "The Memphis Surf Club."

Surfing was brought from Hawaii to Southern California. The sport moved north, sort of by osmosis, and people began coming to our village to try the big waves of Steamer Lane.

A Shore Thing

Surfers would stay in our house, and we'd stay in theirs during our surfing safaris to the south. We'd get the better

ON BOARD. The author (above) exited Steamer Lane with his surfboard as he passed the "Traditional Rules of Surfing" sign (right) posted by nearby Santa Cruz's parks office.

TRADITIONAL RULES OF SURFING

FIRST SURFER ON WAVE HAS RIGHT OF WAY

PADDLE AROUND WAVE NOT THROUGH IT

HANG ON TO YOUR BOARD HELP FELLOW SURFER

BY SAM REID

CITY OF SANTA CRUZ

PARKS & RECREATION

THE SURF crashes against a sea wall as people sit in their 1950s and 1960s cars to watch surfers out on Monterey Bay at the village of Capitola.

end of the deal, because the water off their beach was 10° warmer.

None of us had any idea that north of our village, outside the small town of Half Moon Bay, were some of the biggest waves in the world—mavericks!

Nothing meant summer as much as the damming of the Soquel River to form "The Lagoon," where the water would warm up in the sun all day. We could swim at night with girls there and have that first kiss as we gazed across the bay to Monterey, sparkling like a charm bracelet on black velvet.

We had no trouble letting go of summer romances because new girls arrived on vacation every 2 weeks. After that, the girls would return to their inland homes and write to the surfers, but few surfers ever wrote back.

Eventually, though, most of us married girls we met on the beach. My wife, Ellen, was a farm girl on vacation from the Sierra foothills. We've been married for more than 40 years.

Life's a Beach

We surfers had nothing in those days, yet we had everything. Clothes, blankets, radios and beer came from beachcombing early in the morning after parties. We ate a lot of peanut butter sandwiches, which seemed to keep us healthy.

Our convertibles and woodies lined a beach sidewalk without parking meters, and 10-foot, multi-colored boards stuck out of our cars like party missiles.

After checking the beach for new girls, we'd paddle out. As we waited for a wave, seals would stick their heads up and sea otters would lie back, inspecting us. When we saw fins break the water, we made sure they belonged to dolphins, which hate sharks and manage to drive them off. We surfed in "The Red Triangle," which had sharks the size of small whales.

There are no words to describe being inside a rolling green barrel of water, feeling a blast of air against your back from the wave collapsing behind you.

The tourists would leave in September, not knowing that the best fog-free weather came in October. The fountains and Skee-Ball parlors would close, and the merry-go-round would be stored in a warehouse. During this best time of the year, we had the beach to ourselves.

Yes, eventually I had to find a job and go to work. I became a college instructor, but I surfed small waves until I was 68.

Regretfully, it's all gone now. Small apartments rent for $1,500 a month and tourists no longer leave at summer's end. There is a year-round traffic jam from urban sprawl, parking is a nightmare and meters greedily swallow quarters.

Oceanfront land became too valuable for merry-go-rounds and concessions. Those innocent amusements and food stands have been replaced with businesses none of us surfers could have afforded to patronize.

Now that I've reached my 70s, it all seems so dreamlike when I look back. Poets write about this, as do songwriters: "Life is but a dream."

Head for the CELLAR!

THIS SHELTER BECAME A NEIGHBORHOOD COMMUNITY CENTER WHEN BAD WEATHER LOOMED DURING THE 1930s.

By Doris Orr, Bastrop, Texas

I have never been in a tornado, but I've spent many hours in a storm cellar escaping from the prospect of such an event.

As a child, I would watch threatening clouds form until they let loose a deluge. That was usually the precise moment our parents would decide we needed to head for shelter. We got soaked doing so, of course.

Our storm cellar became a meeting place for most of our Bryson, Texas, neighborhood during bad weather. We were happy to share our shelter, and, in fact, would have been disappointed if we found out we were the only family who thought it necessary to take cover.

The last one in the cellar closed the door and usually perched on a step. As the kerosene lantern was lit, it revealed canned fruits and vegetables, and jars of jam and jelly lining the crude shelves.

Part of the floor was often covered with new potatoes drying on old newspapers. Smelly onions hung on the walls. Sometimes a spider crawled past, but that was better than the snake I heard was found in someone else's storm cellar.

While we sat out the storm, the conversation usually turned to past storms that those in the cellar, or their parents, had experienced.

Another, more hilarious, topic was the unusual clothing some of the visitors wore to storm cellars.

Dressing in a hurry, and often in the dark, resulted in some strange apparel.

There were stories of people arriving with mismatched shoes or their clothes inside out. My cousin once had a difficult time rushing to get his trousers on, only to discover he was trying to push his legs through his shirt sleeves!

Another story often told was about the bachelor who lived nearby. He always came to the cellar in a storm, but one time, after inventory was taken, we realized he wasn't there.

One of the young men volunteered to go out into the wind and rain to find the man. It turned out he had walked through the wrong gate and ended up in the chicken pen. He had almost climbed the fence looking for the way back out when he was found and led safely to the cellar.

One storm cellar really stands out in my mind. Our family took refuge in it when we were on a fishing trip, an outing that perennially seemed to trigger the biggest storm of the year.

The cellar was so big it could have housed a family for weeks. In fact, we spent the night in it.

I can still hear the water dripping from the eaves and the trees as we emerged after the storm. Frogs were croaking all over.

As children, we were always happy to have had another adventure in the storm cellar.

THANKSGIVING must have been just around the corner when this photo was snapped in 1962. The image is shared by Joe Stabile of Sioux City, Iowa, from a family collection taken before he was born. Marked on the slide is "Cleveland PSA Meeting." The photographer apparently was in town for a Photographic Society of America event and took this picture of the Jones-Russell floral shop.

I had rather be on my farm than be emperor of the world.

—George Washington

Librarian Taught a Lesson

By Lou Gros Louis, Leesburg, Virginia

I grew up in Wilton, New Hampshire, which seemed like a small town right out of a Norman Rockwell painting.

With a population of about 1,300 when I was a kid, it was a close-knit community where people knew each other. My family lived across the street from the town librarian, who taught me a lesson I've never forgotten.

The librarian had an apple orchard containing about 50 trees next to her house. It seemed, in my young boy's estimation, that she always left quite a few apples on the trees. So, one year, my best friend and I hatched a scheme to make some summer money.

We gathered a pile of grocery bags, grabbed my wagon and headed to the orchard. We picked and picked until our bags were full of fruit.

As we were pulling our loaded wagon out of the orchard, whom should we meet but the librarian! She simply asked what we were going to do with all of our apples. We admitted that we'd planned on selling them door to door.

She said that was fine—but that we should come back to her house when all of the apples were sold.

Learning the Hard Way

We thought things had worked out great. We'd return to her house, show her our profit and perhaps enjoy a cold drink for our trouble. A few hours later, our pockets jingling with money, we knocked on her door and were invited in.

The librarian asked how much we'd earned. Emptying our pockets on her kitchen table, we counted $7.50. She then picked up the money and placed it in a jar on a shelf.

"If you boys had asked me for the apples, I would gladly have given them to you to sell, and the money would have been yours," she said. "Because what you did was like stealing, I am going to keep the money and hope you always remember this lesson."

Heads hanging, tired from our work and upset at losing our hard-earned money, we trudged home with my empty wagon in tow. It was quite a hard lesson for two young boys.

Several years later, when my friend and I were in high school, we needed to visit the library to write a paper. While there, we saw the librarian approach us.

Thinking she was going to yell at us for talking too loudly, we waited for the scolding. Instead, she placed a $5 bill in front of each of us.

"Do you remember when you picked my apples and sold them without permission, and I took your money?" she asked. We nodded our heads.

"I saved the money, with interest, to give back to you one day. You visit the library often, and I thought this would be a good time. I'm sure you both will be fine men someday," she added.

We were stunned. Not only had this gracious woman given us money that she'd saved for us for years, but she let us know that she still had faith and confidence in us.

I've thought of this lesson many times in my life, as I went on to become an Eagle Scout, serve in the Korean War and hold positions in local government.

This could only have happened in a town so reflective of Americana, one that created a foundation that has guided me throughout my life.

the happiest
years of my life

LOS ANGELES WAS JUST ANOTHER PLACE FOR
NEIGHBORHOOD KIDS TO ENJOY GROWING UP.

By Richard Cabrera, Falcon Heights, Minnesota

Los Angeles is often seen as a city of glamour and excitement, centering around Hollywood. Others see a dangerous place, filled with gangs and violence.

To me, at age 8, in 1949, it was home, the place where new things happened daily.

We lived near the corner of Fourth and Soto Streets. It's in Boyle Heights, a neighborhood that, at the time, was like a place from the Our Gang movies. We had a happy population of Mexican, Japanese, Russian and Jewish families.

In complete safety, my pals and I roamed and played around our streets, never more than three or four blocks from home. Some of my happiest years were spent on those streets.

Our gang of kids, all five of us from diverse backgrounds, would hang out at the candy store on Fourth Street. The proprietor, a gentle old man, sometimes let us take more candy than our pennies would buy.

In summer, he'd give us ice chunks from his icebox to cool us as we sat in front of the store reading his 10-cent comic books.

I recall one of the store's better treats was a dill pickle, not from the barrel, but dipped in green wax and costing a dime. Half the treat was biting off the wax and chewing it first before eating the pickle.

We were all together as much as possible. As I remember it, we never got into major trouble, and we had some great experiences for city kids.

Early in 1949, we got a big surprise. I woke one morning to my father telling me to look outside. I did and saw something I had never seen before—snow!

It had snowed in the center of Los Angeles for the first time in most memories. It was only an inch or two, but we got the greatest enjoyment out of it that we could. We built a snowman and threw snowballs until it all melted. We even ate the snow. It was clean as could be, with no smog in those days to dirty it.

Grandma to the Rescue

Another fun pastime for us was walking on a neighbor's wall, balancing as if in a circus act. The wall bordered a lawn and wasn't more than 4 feet high, but to us, it was enormous.

One time, I lost my balance and fell on the sidewalk. It knocked the wind out of me and split my chin, which bled all over the place.

The gang panicked but helped me, as if I was a wounded warrior, to my grandmother's house next door. Grandma, who spoke only Spanish,

YOUNG SWEETHEARTS. The author and his first girlfirend, Rosie Mandel, are shown in 1948.

calmly tended to me. There was a hospital across the street, but she applied a bandage and kept me on the sofa for a day to recuperate.

Today, I'd have had stitches, but in 1949, her care was enough, and I have a nice scar on my chin to remind me.

Grandma also gave me one of my proudest childhood moments. An avid reader, I'd often be taken to the local library. My folks were working one day when I told Grandma I wanted to go to the library when they got home.

She had a better idea. It was time, Grandma said, that I learned to go to the library on my own.

I knew the way and it was safe to walk there, but Grandma gave me bus tokens for the trip. So,

at the age of 8, I set out on an adventure.

Alone, I took the bus up Soto to First Street, then proudly stepped onto a Red Line trolley to travel down First Street to the Benjamin Franklin Library (it's still there).

I recall the friendly conductor asking where I was going and helping me make my stop. Looking at it now, I don't think I went more than 10 blocks, but for an 8-year-old boy, it was a grand trip. And the gang all thought it was a swell thing, too.

Those were the best of times. My friends and I spent 4 or 5 happy years together, until my parents built a house in the suburbs on the GI Bill.

Los Angeles was safe, clean and a great place for me and my gang to grow up. I do miss those days.

THE CITY OF ANGELS

A moment in wartime was captured in this nostalgic 1942 picture, taken in the 300 West block of Eighth Street at South Broadway in Los Angeles, California.

The photograph comes from the Joseph Blackstock Collection and is shared by Joseph's son, Forrest Blackstock of Kingman, Arizona.

Signs of the time in the bustling city are many. Along the right side of the picture is a marquee promoting a wartime newsreel and a sign with an arrow pointing to an air-raid shelter.

In the foreground are several men wearing military garb.

The commercial establishments on the right side of the street include the Lankershim Hotel, the Pig 'n' Whistle restaurant, Los Angeles Furniture, the Schwabacher-Frey Company and Crosby Jewelers.

At left, by the jam-packed sidewalk, are the Mayflower Restaurant, with its "tested quality donuts" and Maxwell House coffee. Behind the streetlamp in front of the Leed's sign is a traffic light with moving stop-and-go signs.

'Getting Wired' in Rural America

By Jack Barnes, East Lansing, Michigan

During my early years in the 1920s and 1930s, most farmers were dependent upon kerosene or gasoline lamps for lighting. We were no exception.

Our Coldwater, Michigan, neighbors, the Ogdens, were really lording it over us with two ultramodern contraptions—an old Fordson tractor and a Delco lighting system.

Their lighting system consisted of a generator and a series of batteries to power electric lights. Out in the country, it was quite a marvel.

When President Franklin D. Roosevelt took office during the Great Depression, he announced his New Deal programs, including one for rural electrification. Many rural electric cooperatives were formed. Where they weren't formed, power companies felt the pressure to build lines and electrify rural America.

How well I remember when Consumers Power Company started planning to put an electrical line down our road. Everybody wanted the electricity, but all the farmers wanted the lines, poles and guy wires on the other side of the road so they wouldn't have to farm around them.

Our line came down our side of the road.

As the plans became reality, there was a big rush to get wired—no easy trick in those old farmhouses.

Harry Thompson, a farmer located west of us, was a member of our church who had somehow learned about wiring, and he did ours for us.

LIFE ON THE FARM. In this picture taken in 1938, the 17-year-old author is leading a cow, one of his animals for his 4-H club.

Of course, the main thing was lights. That's what we all talked about.

How exciting it was that day in the mid-1930s when the juice was turned on. Lights suddenly came on up and down the road—houses, barns, henhouses, yard lights. Wherever there were lights, they were on.

Lights were the preoccupation, but salesmen soon followed. It wasn't long before we all had electric radios to take the place of the ones run off storage batteries that always seemed to run down.

Soon after the radios came electric irons, washing machines, refrigerators, stoves...the list went on. One of our firsts was an electric motor to run the pump jack to pump water at the barn.

Then Mom got a washer; no more pushing that darned gasoline engine from the barn to the house and back every washday.

In my mind, nothing ever had or ever will change the face of rural America as much or as fast as those electric lights did. Every farm kid who lived during the Great Depression era remembers the day the lights came on.

Pennsylvania Pride

DIGNITARIES. "The truck driver in this 1939 Armistice Day parade held in Beaver, Pennsylvania, is my father, Harry E. Watterson," relates Jack Watterson from Suntree, Florida. "Also in the fire truck is Dan Moore, who was Beaver's mayor and the town's volunteer fire chief. Both Dad and my younger brother, Gene, served more than 50 years on the Beaver Volunteer Fire Department."

BICENTENNIAL CELEBRATION. In this 1955 photo, William Lewallen posed with his daughters in front of their residence in Middletown, Pennsylvania. "I'm the 5-year-old on the left, and my 6-year-old sister Karen is on the right," says Cheryl Brightbill, who lives in Palmyra. "My dad belonged to Middletown's Rescue Hose Co. #3 Firehouse and was about to march in the town's bicentennial parade. My grandmother, Bertha Lewallen, made my sister and me the patriotic outfits we wore for the occasion."

A great city is that which has the greatest men and women.

—Walt Whitman

NEW BUDDIES. Joe held up a cat for a photo with the author's mother, Margaret Carroll, on the Carroll farm in the 1920s.

Second Home On The Farm

'FRESH AIR FUND' BOY BECAME PART OF THE FAMILY.

By David Carroll, Verona, Virginia

Before my parents had any children of their own, they took in an unknown child who lived hundreds of miles away.

They signed up for the Fresh Air Fund, a program that gives inner-city kids the chance to experience country life by attending summer camp or by spending summer vacations with volunteer host families.

In 1927, my mom and dad, Margaret and John Carroll, drove from our home in Weyers Cave, Virginia, to Staunton to pick up a boy named Joe. He had traveled on an open-car train from New York City, where he lived in an area known as "Hell's Kitchen."

Seven-year-old Joe was sooty from the train smoke. After his bath, my folks were surprised to find he was white!

My parents hosted Joe through the Fresh Air Fund for the next 10 summers, during which

time some interesting things happened…like when he tried to be helpful and picked all the green tomatoes in the garden.

Another time, Mom was going to town to sell eggs. She got Joe ready and told him to wait for her to get dressed. When Mom came out, she found him sitting in the basket of now broken eggs.

When she asked why he was sitting there, Joe said, "Mrs. Carroll, you told me if a chicken set on eggs, they would hatch little chickens. I thought I could hatch little chickens."

Joe loved to go to lawn parties, but because of Mom and Dad's accent, he thought they were going to an "alarm party."

By Train or Bike

When Joe was 17 and too old to come as a Fresh Air child, he found his way to our house

on his own. He rode his bicycle all the way from New York City—a trip of about 400 miles! We still have a newspaper clipping about his journey.

During the trip, Joe had stopped in Pennsylvania and milked a cow to pay for his supper. After about a week, his mother called my parents to ask if he was there.

For 2 years, Joe came on his bike. The next year, he drove down in a Model A and brought along his new wife, Ethel, for their honeymoon.

Ethel had never been out of New York City. Her new experience in the country included a walk in the pasture and use of the outdoor toilet. What a way to spend a honeymoon!

Joe and Ethel came almost every year for their vacation. They brought their baby daughter, Barbara, and a few years later their son, Gary.

When Dad died in 1959, Joe told his boss that he had kin in Virginia and needed time off to attend the funeral.

Joe worked for the New York transit system and made a good life for himself. His daughter became a teacher and his son an eye doctor.

Trip to New York

In 1964, I visited Joe and his family in New York City for the first time. Joe took me all over the city that week. We went to the World's Fair, and he showed me the shops that were going to be torn down to make room for the two tallest buildings in the world—the Twin Towers.

When I got married in 1966, Joe and his family came for my wedding. Joe was just like family. He was Jewish and we were Protestant, but it made no difference to any of us. He'd even attend church with us when he visited.

When his daughter got married, we went to New York for the wedding. This was our first Jewish wedding—a beautiful occasion. We were seated at the most honored table, and a lot of people wanted to know who we were.

In later years, Joe and his wife would visit every Thanksgiving. Eventually, we began to see that his health was failing.

One year, before Thanksgiving, Barbara called and said her parents would not be able to come. About 2 weeks later, we received a call saying Joe had died. My wife and I went to New York to sit shivah with the family.

Joe always said that the Fresh Air Fund and my family meant so much to him. He meant a lot to us, too. So much so that my wife, Vicky, and I became actively involved in the Fresh Air Fund program, both as leaders and escorts back and forth to New York.

In fact, we hosted a "Fresh Air grandchild," the daughter of a child we'd taken in for years. I think Joe would have been proud.

Red Brick Building Block

BRONX BUDDIES LEFT NEIGHBORHOOD WITH FRIENDSHIPS AND FOND MEMORIES.

By Eydie Scher, Sparks, Nevada

Mohegan Avenue, sandwiched between 175th and 176th Streets, was a quick hop to Crotona Park and the main thoroughfares of Tremont Avenue and Southern Boulevard. On one side were private residences. On our side were apartment buildings, of which ours was the largest.

Many years of my life as Edith Bram, in the 1940s and 1950s, were spent in that red brick New York building. Surrounding it was a huge, concreted courtyard protected by two massive, marble, animal-like statues. We used to hop on them and ride off into imaginative oblivion.

The sound of the hallway buzzer meant that the dumbwaiter had arrived with my mother's groceries. I would poke my head through the opening, watch the dumbwaiter descend four floors through the darkened abyss and call out a thank-you to the tobacco-chewing, white-bearded superintendent below.

Our super, "Old Louie," was someone who had a crackling voice and an unsmiling face. He always dressed in dirty denim overalls and seemed to live in the basement among the bicycles, washing machines and trash.

Fun for All Seasons

The orange- and black-flecked fire escape was our summer retreat; we picnicked under the lines of laundry swaying in the breeze. Two flights down lived my best friend. We'd scamper up and down the two flights and knock on each other's windows.

My other very best friend lived in the center building on the first floor, and we're still friends today. Many of us remain Bronx buddies, even though we now live in different places

Sometimes, the fire hydrants emptied their contents into the tarred street, dousing delighted hordes of barefoot kids who sought relief from the scorching summers. We'd sometimes head up to the tar beach—the roof—a ridiculous place to be on a hot summer day, but you couldn't retreat to any air-conditioning!

Wintry weather sent us scurrying to the snowy hills of Crotona Park with our sleds or to frozen Indian Lake, where we first learned to ice-skate. When we got home, we'd scrunch our feet under the radiator to thaw. It hissed and sprayed steam at us but did warm us up.

Stickball, skelzy and ring-a-levio in the middle of the street were our favorite pastimes. Cars intruding on our territory were scorned.

Changing Landscape

As the 1950s came and went, the neighborhood changed. We moved to an apartment in Yonkers, to a new building with an elevator and even a pool. It was an area of fine schools, fine people and a fine environment for children.

I met my Navy husband at the apartment pool while I was still in high school. Less than 3 years later, we moved back to the Bronx. In 1966, we left the Bronx forever and moved into our first house in Rockland County.

The red brick apartment building of my youth is gone. When I returned to the block, a pile of rubble was the only remaining evidence that the building existed on Mohegan Avenue.

However, its image remains in my mind. You can never truly go back home, but the neighborhood is our heritage. The Bronx no longer beckons, but it is fondly kept in my memories!

come meet
my new girl

"In this photograph, I'm holding the hand of a friend on a farm located near Holland, Michigan, in 1956," explains Randall Vandenberg of Flagstaff, Arizona. "The girl's father owned the farm. The snapshot makes me wonder if I was waving at the cows in the fenced-in pasture!"

CHAPTER 9

the Spirit of YOUTH

With plenty of pluck and spunk, American youngsters have celebrated their heritage and carried on traditions while making their way in an ever-changing nation.

"Children who attended small rural schools years ago faced more challenges than just classroom studies," notes Rita Schloegel of Lewiston, Minnesota.

"The teacher in our one-room school near Wetonka, South Dakota, in the 1930s and early 1940s taught all eight grades. There was no school bus, janitor or lunch program. We didn't even have running water—each student brought a bottle of their own for drinking.

"We all shared in the work that went with keeping the school clean and were assigned tasks at monthly meetings. Younger children cleaned the erasers and blackboards while older students carried coal for the heating stove and swept the floor.

"Most of those small rural schools are now gone. But when I got to high school, I noticed that many of the students from those country schools were at the head of the class at graduation."

Page through this chapter for more stories of the young generations who inherited America.

page 201

page 194

page 202

page 190

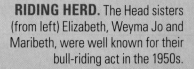

The Rodeo Girls

IT WAS A REAL BULL STORY WHEN CHORES TURNED INTO FUN AND PROFIT.

By Maribeth Bryant, Greenville, Texas

Many farmers and ranchers give bulls a wide berth, and for good reason. But two of my sisters and I didn't shy away from these big, intimidating animals. In fact, we rode and performed on them.

We grew up on a farm in Campbell, Hunt County, Texas, with three other siblings. Our cows, chickens, turkeys, hogs and 2-acre garden were our income and food supply sources.

My siblings and I would milk the cows every morning before heading off to school. In the afternoon, after chores, we had our "fun time" with the bulls.

We'd each get a bull calf and play with him, then have a contest to see who could ride one. This playing eventually turned into training the bulls for riding.

Our cows were moved from one pasture to another daily. After the bulls we'd trained got larger, we'd drive the herd, riding the bulls, as we headed to school.

We'd ride the bulls or a cow like horses to the edge of our property, then get off and walk to Twin Elm School.

In the afternoon, we'd catch the bulls and, while riding them, herd the cows back to the barn for milking. In summer, we spent many hours training the animals by moonlight before being called into the house for bedtime.

A STUNT called the "lying head stand" is rehearsed by three of the Head sisters in this photo taken at their Texas farm.

After we trained them to ride, we decided to try to teach them tricks, and we did.

Taking the Bull by the Horns

The animals became a part of our life and entertainment. Swimming was one activity we enjoyed with them. The bulls would swim across the pool—a 1-acre, dammed-up pond—with us on their backs. When we reached the middle, we'd dismount, catch their tails and let them drag us across.

If you missed the tail, it was bad news; that was how we learned to swim.

Jumping ditches while riding the bulls was another fun pastime. With water flowing, we'd see which bull could jump the widest ditch.

We also had races riding the bulls. Since I'm writing this, I'll say my bull always won!

About twice a month, we had a 3-mile cattle drive using the bulls instead of horses. We didn't use bridles or saddles, just a small quirt.

Mom and Dad didn't know about the "bullfights" we occasionally had. We made them very short because we didn't want our animals or us to get hurt.

Our fun started becoming serious business when neighbors and friends began asking us to perform for them. My older sister Weyma Jo, twin sister Elizabeth and I became a specialty act—the Three Head Sisters and their Highly Trained Herefords.

I was on "Bullie," nearly 1,600 pounds; Elizabeth rode "Little Bull," 1,350 pounds; and Weyma Jo rode "Wo Jo," an 1,100-pound cow. We had a substitute bull, "Snickles," that was used when Wo Jo was pregnant.

Our brother, who also had a bull that was trained to ride, passed away in 1946.

We were invited to perform in the Lone Oak Rodeo in 1950, and it seemed to us as if all of Hunt, Rains and Hopkins Counties turned out to watch.

TERRIFIC TRICK. The Head sisters (from back to front), Weyma Jo, Maribeth and Elizabeth, demonstrate the triple stand, one of the stunts they performed in their popular rodeo shows.

It was the first time the bulls had ever been under bright lights, and they were great. This was the first of our several amateur shows.

Star Attraction

In 1951, we joined the Rodeo Cowboy Association, where all the big shows were. Within 3 years, we had performed in shows in Oklahoma, Arkansas, Louisiana and Texas, including the Fort Worth Fat Stock Rodeo and the weekly Texas Prison Rodeo.

Our shows each ran about 15 minutes, and we'd do the triple stand, with Bullie's front feet on a pedestal and us standing on his back. We also did a kneeling act, a crawling act under the bulls and an act where each of us stood on an animal's back.

Our mother traveled with us and made all our costumes. She continued our schooling and made sure we were able to attend church.

Our act could have remained on the road continuously; however, Dad, our manager, thought that work on the farm had to go on.

After nearly 4 years of performing, I decided to get married, without thinking of what would happen to our act. We performed only a few times after that, because I moved away.

One day, Dad asked me what I wanted to do with my bull. I told Dad to sell him, and this was my greatest regret. If I had it to do over, I would have kept him for the rest of his life.

None are so old as those who have outlived enthusiasm.

—Henry David Thoreau

Armed & Ready

CHORES BEAT ATTITUDE WHEN A BULLYING BOY GOT A BIG SURPRISE.

By Helen Marie Bentz, Hartly, Delaware

As a teenager, I complained about having to do farm work. Later, I realized how much of a benefit it was—especially when it came to dealing with an obnoxious boy.

My father, Homer Goldsborough, bought a farm east of Smyrna, Georgia, before he married my mother, Miriam Montgomery, and that's where I spent my childhood.

When my brother Roger and I were older, there was always work to be done. We learned to drive by taking our father's dump truck through the open fields.

All through our teen years, as soon as we got off the school bus, we changed our clothes and started farm chores.

When I was in the seventh grade, in 1963, a big boy about my age but double my size loved to give me trouble. He would pass me in the school hallway, hit me in the arm and run.

I didn't tell my parents about it because they did business with the boy's parents, who owned a roadside stand for selling produce.

By lifting a lot of heavy things while doing my farm work, I was getting strong. But I had no idea just how strong until the day when the big boy

A PETITE STATURE concealed the strength of the author in these photos. She is pictured with her brother in 1953 (above) and in her sixth-grade portrait (left) in 1962.

from school came to my house with his mother.

The boy was sitting at the kitchen table with his mother, along with a smart attitude, and he wanted to arm-wrestle me. At first I turned him down, but he persisted, so I agreed.

Much to my amazement and that of our parents and the boy, I proved to be an equal match for him. He wasn't able to pin my arm down, and the contest continued. When I was about ready to give up and let him win, he gave up. I had won!

The boy was really embarrassed that I, a girl half his size, was able to beat him. He never hit my arm again when he passed me in school.

What he never knew was that, after the match, my mother ended up taking me to the doctor for pulled muscles in my wrestling arm.

GO TEAM!

GIRLS' SOFTBALL WAS A HIT

Before the days of organized softball leagues for girls, I played sandlot baseball every summer with the boys in my Galesburg, Illinois, neighborhood.

Then one day in 1959, when I was 14, Dad and I were watching a Yankees game on TV. He looked up from his newspaper to tell me a girls' fast-pitch softball team was being formed called the Galesburg Scrappers—sponsored by McCabe Scrap Iron.

Our city Little League teams allowed only boys to play, so this was my chance to play with a real team.

Dad took me to the tryouts, and after a week or so, I was chosen! I played first base or right field, depending on whether the starting first baseman was pitching.

Our team's coach, Bill Costello, chewed tobacco and had a peg leg that creaked when he walked. We never dared to ask him what had happened, but there were many theories.

At one game, we didn't have enough players to field a team. My mom and my 10-year-old sister were in the stands watching, and we got them down to play. When the three of us came up to bat, we each got a home run.

The Scrappers traveled a 50-mile radius to such towns as Monmouth, Canton, Kewanee and Toulon. Once we drove all the way to Dwight to play the women's penitentiary team.

I remember we all had to walk through the security area to be frisked. I was so intimidated by it that to this day, I can't recall which team won the game.

I played with the Scrappers from 1958 to 1961, and the experience remains one of my fondest memories of summertime fun.

— *Marcia Callahan Johnson, Galesburg, Illinois*

NOT JUST FOR BOYS. This 1960 photo shows the Scrappers of Galesburg, Illinois, who included (front row, from left) Sandy Banks, Rosa Faro, Jan Burquin, the author, Celia Shugart, Ellie Shugart, Mary Mallin, (back row, from left) an unidentified player, Liz Shy, Mary Davis, Connie Daniels, Ina Davis and Bill Costello.

FIERCE RUNNER. "My father, Doug Harris, is running the ball through the line in this photo from 1944, when he was a 16-year-old football player for East Nashville High School," writes Terry Harris of Smyrna, Tennessee. "The blocker to the left is Tom Keysaer. The blocker in the foreground is Richard Fulton, a former U.S. congressman and later a popular mayor of Nashville. My dad said the white-colored football was more easily seen during night games, and the leather helmets had no face masks. Football in the 1940s was tough."

SWEET VICTORY

Small-town high school basketball really heated up our long, cold winters in Northern Illinois, as evidenced by the photograph above.

It shows the DeKalb Township High School cheering section on February 6, 1951. I took the picture while a student at DeKalb.

The scene is an exciting game between two archrivals, the DeKalb Barbs and the Sycamore Spartans. Earlier in the 1950-1951 basketball season, Sycamore had defeated the Barbs in DeKalb by a score of 31-29.

Tension was high for this game, and many DeKalb basketball fans made the 5-mile trip to the Spartans' gymnasium in Sycamore. DeKalb ended up prevailing in this game, 49-45, and revenge was sweet!

The cheerleaders shown are, from left, Barbara Ballard (with her back to the camera), Dette Meineke, Sharon Wilcox, Norma McLean, Susan Stefani and Faith Ebbesen.

The ballplayers I could remember are, from left, Jack Vogeler, Bob Cortelyou, David Hoppe, Jack Boardman, Ron Massier and Don Cook.

—*John George, Pleasant Hill, California*

SPIRIT SQUAD. These high school cheerleaders showed plenty of pep at Addison Central School in Addison, New York, during the early 1950s. "My aunt, Shirley Cornell Wright, is shown on the far right," writes Linda Conpenelis Schmidt of East Bethany, New York. "The maroon and gray uniforms were made of satin."

my first car

PLAN TO SHOW OFF NEW WHEELS CAME UP FLAT.

By Sanford Morris, Los Angeles, California

I stood proudly with one foot on the running board of my new 1934 Ford coupe. At age 16, I felt grown up at last.

No longer would I have to depend on anyone else to drive me. I had scraped together $350 to buy this car from my cousin, and even though it was 12 years old, it was brand-new to me.

In fact, I felt like hot stuff with my sporty wheels that boasted twin exhaust pipes, special hubcaps, a shade in the rear window and a push-button starter on the dashboard. Now, all I had to do was show it off!

My excitement grew as I planned my first drive to school. In my imagination, everyone stopped to admire my car as I cruised slowly past the front of the building.

I even daydreamed about that first trip to school resembling a movie premiere. Drums would roll to announce me, and shining beams would put me in the spotlight!

To get ready, I polished the car until I could see my reflection—a very happy face.

Debut Dud

When the big day finally arrived, I could barely wait to head to school. Feeling proud and important, I drove off and slowly approached the front of the school building, my twin exhaust pipes purring.

But something was wrong. The area was deserted. Where was everyone?

I soon realized what had happened—the bell had already rung! I was too late. Not a soul was there to witness the debut of my new ride.

It was as if I'd come to a party looking like a million dollars, and no one was there to see me. I felt cheated and disappointed.

Being in the middle of those awkward teenage years, I didn't focus on the fact that I would still have the chance to show off my car. And I would be just as proud and thrilled as I thought I'd be.

After that first letdown, I had many great times and adventures with my old Ford coupe. The car proved to be an endless source of happiness for me.

When I got married, I sold my prize possession for $95. How I'd love to have it back!

In the Scouts

NOT A BADGE OUT OF PLACE. "Mrs. Lorene Spencer is pictured at her Iowa City home, in 1951, with (from left) daughters Janis, Jane, June and Judy," writes Max Abildtrup of The Villages, Florida. "They were dressing in their Girl Scout uniforms to have their picture taken by the local newspaper, the *Iowa Press Citizen*. Mrs. Spencer was their Girl Scout leader. The girls' father, Norman, was the Conoco distributor in town. The girl on the far right was my wife of 46 years before passing away in 2006. The remaining sisters are still close, continuing their longtime tradition of traveling together at least once a year."

WITH THE BOYS—AND GIRLS

My dad, Ernest Neimeyer, joined Boy Scout Troop 70 of St. John's Lutheran Church in Emmaus, Pennsylvania, in the late 1930s. He was in the Flying Eagle patrol with six other boys.

By the early 1940s, citizens were asked to save gasoline for the war effort, so hiking was popular. During the 1942 camping season, Scouts who hiked to and from Camp Trexler were given a 66-mile patch. If you only hiked to the camp, you received a 33-mile patch.

Everyone in Dad's patrol received the 33-mile patch for hiking to camp. They also endured two days of suffering, plenty of blisters and a lot of ragging because they didn't hike back as well!

Members of Dad's patrol had their picture in the newspaper for participating in a drill that involved finding a lost man. Several of the older members were even made honorary Girl Scouts after attending the girls' meetings and teaching them scouting skills.

Blisters and all, being a Boy Scout was a great experience Dad always looked back on fondly.

—*David Neimeyer, Fogelsville, Pennsylvania*

A RIP-ROARING TIME

The day after Christmas in 1947, when I was 8 years old, several friends and I acted out the Clement C. Moore poem *The Night Before Christmas* at my Girl Scout troop party.

The role of Santa was assigned to Rita, a tomboy with a devilish sense of adventure. Dressed in a crepe-paper Santa suit, a beard of cotton and a stocking cap, her role was to hide in our cardboard fireplace until the right moment.

As I read the line, "Down the chimney St. Nicholas came," I expected Rita to pop out. When nothing happened, I repeated the line, which still brought no result. I walked to the fireplace and whispered for Rita to come out, but she said, "No, I ripped my pants!"

I apologized to the audience of Scouts, parents and siblings and finished my reading. Rita refused to come out until the lights went out!

—*Joan Peidl, Spring Hill, Florida*

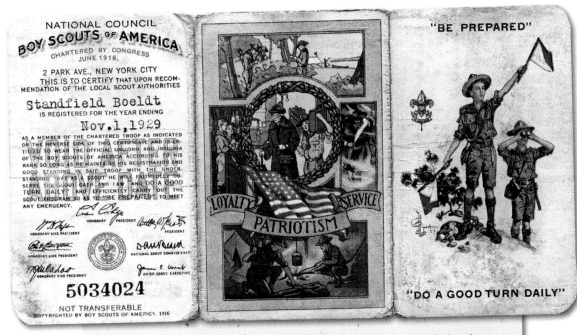

SPECIAL MEMENTO. "This Boy Scouts membership card (above), dated November 1, 1929, is one of the few keepsakes my father left," relates Jack Boeldt of Indianapolis, Indiana. "My dad, Standfield Boeldt, was a man of deeds, not things. Mom was a Cub Scout den mother during World War II, and I have had many active years in the Scouts. I have so many good memories of those times."

holiday high jinks

SPACE-AGE CHRISTMAS.
Michael (left) and Patrick Pfeiffer, ages 4 and 6 in 1961, were ready for takeoff in their cardboard Mercury space capsules, in Longmeadow, Massachusetts. "My husband, Jack, and I were up most of the night using paper clips to keep these together," says the boys' mom, Joan Pfeiffer from Upland, California. "I remember using a grapefruit and orange to show Patrick how the capsules orbited the Earth. The boys still say it was the best Christmas."

HALLOWEEN HOBO.
After trick-or-treating, Robert Gouveia proudly displayed his loot. "This late-1950s photo shows me back at our Boston home, ready to dig in to all the candy," he writes from Burlington, Massachusetts.

"Any fruit 'n' cereal starts tongues waggin' ...as long as it's Post Raisin Bran"

"...and Suzie—it's the only cereal with sugar on the raisins. And listen, the television said more people eat Post Raisin Bran than any other kind. Well, gotta go now—can't talk and eat at the same time. Bye-ee!"

"ALL POST CEREALS HAPPEN TO BE JUST A LITTLE BIT BETTER"

The Breakfast Foods of General Foods

Head of the Class

STYLISH STANDOFF

When I was in the sixth grade in 1954, one of my classes was home economics. Our teacher, Mrs. Bates, informed us at the beginning of the year that we were old enough to learn how to act like young ladies.

Mrs. Bates didn't like the fact that some of the girls wore jeans to school. One day, she strongly suggested that we show up the next morning in dresses.

Several of the girls followed her advice. But a few of us, including me, arrived in our usual jeans.

It was the beginning of a nine-month standoff, with Mrs. Bates, who intended to turn us all into proper ladies, on one side and a few 11-year-olds, who wanted no part of the world of fancy outfits, curlers and nail polish, on the other.

Mrs. Bates tried her best. She lectured us on how to choose clothing that matched.

"Don't wear colors that clash," she said. "Don't ever wear a plaid with a stripe. Make sure your clothes are clean and pressed. Wrinkled clothing is unacceptable. Shoes should be polished." The list went on and on.

Because my mother had already taught me these very rules, I was often bored in class, and Mrs. Bates would catch me daydreaming.

"Mary Ann, are you listening?" she asked. "Are you taking proper notes? If you aren't, you'll fail the next test."

Instead of failing, I made perfect scores. This baffled Mrs. Bates.

Each day, one student had a special lunch with Mrs. Bates in the Home Ec room. When it was my turn, I wore a nice dress and my Sunday shoes.

She was very pleased and asked, "Now, don't you feel like a proper young lady?" I said I did. After lunch, she manicured my fingernails.

The next day, I was back in jeans. Mrs. Bates was polite and never voiced her disappointment.

After lessons on etiquette and cooking, it was time to learn to sew. We had to bring a pattern, material and notions so we could make a dress using the classroom sewing machines.

Mom and I picked out a pattern, a pretty dress with scallops at the neckline and waist. The fabric was blue polished cotton.

Mrs. Bates tactfully said that the pattern was too difficult for a first try and offered to help me. I didn't tell her that my mother was a professional seamstress and I already knew how to sew!

On the last day of school, we had a fashion show. We paraded in our dresses and passed out our baked-in-class cookies to our audience, the boys from shop class.

And then the school year was over. Back home again, I promptly changed into my jeans for the summer. Sorry, Mrs. Bates.

— *Mary Ann Gove*
Cottonwood, Arizona

We cannot always build the future for our youth, but we can build our youth for the future.

—*Franklin D. Roosevelt*

LANDSCAPE ARTISTS. Onstage with Agassiz School art instructor Kathryn Pease (at bottom right), in June 1944, were eighth graders (from left) Warren Schultz, Donald Schuler, Mabel Nixon, Frances Burgess, Luella Jachim (author), Betty Corrigan and Bill Dunst. Luella wore a maroon-and-white school ribbon.

A+ ACTIVITIES

As the third generation of my family to attend Agassiz School, at 2851 N. Seminary Ave., Chicago, I walked about five blocks to school every morning, then home for lunch and then back to school.

I loved school, and as an eighth grader, in 1943-1944, I patrolled the playground at recess as a Red Belt. We stopped fights or name-calling, made sure the children behaved and took into the gym or office anyone who got hurt.

The Red Belts also diligently patrolled the invisible line between the girls' and boys' sides. ("Boys Entrance" and "Girls Entrance" are still engraved on the building.)

During "Clean-Up Week" each spring, we heard talks from a fire marshal on the dangers of fire and how to look for junk under stairways and in basements. Posters were made saying, "Clean Up," "Paint Up" and "Light Up," and we marched around the block with our signs.

Every morning, we pledged allegiance to the flag and sang *The Star-Spangled Banner* as our eighth-grade teacher, Miss Gertrude Houlahan, played the piano. On D-Day, June 6, 1944, we were all very solemn and showed our respect with prayers and a special assembly.

Every graduating class had a huge play or presentation. Ours involved the life of Stephen Foster. We sang, soft-shoed, spoke parts and painted a fabulous backdrop of an old-time steamboat and landing dock.

I often wonder about my classmates from those days. I can still picture every one of them.

—*Luella Knudsen, Batavia, Illinois*

READY FOR LEARNING

Smiles were mixed with somewhat embarrassed looks on the fresh, young faces of these 1956-1957 first graders in Jacksonville, Florida.

More than 50 years have passed since the curly-headed girl on the far left was in first grade at Spring Park Elementary School. That little girl with the Toni-in-the-box curls is me, sitting next to my classmate Gayle.

As I look at this photo, it's hard to believe that these youngsters are now in their 60s!

The woman sitting on the left was our teacher, Anita Horton. I can't recall for sure, but I think the woman standing must have been an aide.

I would walk down our street and through the woods to and from school with my sisters, now Mary Champney and Patti Lambert. We are the daughters of Buddy and Barbara Bardon.

Our mother served as a crossing guard where our street ended and the woods began. We three girls felt very proud and special having Mom there to be sure that all of the neighborhood children crossed the street safely.

And children continue walking to Spring Park Elementary School, which still stands at 2250 Spring Park Road in Jacksonville.

—*Cathy Bardon Knight, Green Cove Springs, Florida*

BANNER YEAR. "This photo was taken in 1926 in front of Sunbury High School. Sunbury is located about 50 miles north of Harrisburg, Pennsylvania," says Willard "Bill" Busler, who now resides in Harrisburg. "I'm the boy holding the banner—I had just won the city's third-grade spelling championship. At the time, there were nine third-grade classes in Sunbury. I went all the way through high school with a lot of these same kids." Although he was a fine speller, Bill did not follow a writing career but rather got a job with the Navy and eventually designed machines.

CRISP SHEETING. Precise work was taught in this sheet-metal club at P.S. 51, in Bronx, New York. "The teacher in the lab coat is Alfred Frank, a relative of mine," explains James Moseman of Fleischmanns. "This photograph is from the spring term of 1942. There was a sign above the blackboard that read, 'Careless Workers Lose Their Jobs; Only Careful Workers Wanted Here.'"

Off to School

A HOMEMADE BUS was full of Bratton Union School kids in Richardson County, Nebraska, including (from left) two unknown kids, John Wilkinson, Weldon Reagan, Luella Aden, Leon Remmers, Lorene Hector, Marjorie Lampe, Wayne Lampe, Duward Meyers, Armond Reagan and Bob Mehlin. Armond is the brother-in-law of Cleveland, Tennessee's Bill Beck, who sent the circa-1939 photo.

DARING TO BE SEEN. "These teen lovebirds walking to school together in 1938, were my mom and dad, Doris Foster and R.L. King," shares Peggy McClain of Mount Pleasant, Tennessee. "The 16-year-olds were on their way to Hay Long High School in Mount Pleasant. They were sweethearts all through high school and, of course, later married and had my sister, Shelby, and me."

SAFETY FIRST. On a snowy winter's day in Batavia, New York, a crossing guard safely guided Donald Schmidt across the street from Spruce Street Elementary School. "I was in kindergarten when this photo was taken in 1955," he writes from East Bethany, New York.

May Day Reign

FAIREST OF THE FESTIVAL.
"My sister, Betty Ann Panton Wheatley (middle), was Queen of the May, on May Day 1938, in Alameda, California," relates Charlotte Isabel Calder of Paso Robles. "I'm on the right. We don't recall who the other girl was."

SPRING ROYALTY.
"This photograph shows me as the 1947 May Day king at Beaumont Grammar School, in Knoxville, Tennessee," says Bobby Wise of Traverse City, Michigan. "After marching into the gym, I put the crown on the queen, Nancy Jo Jollay. Then we sat and watched a stage show. The flag bearer on the far left is Jerry Van Hoozier."

FAST FRIENDS. Barbara Courtright notes that Dean (right), the long-distance bicyclist, and her son, Mike, hit it off right away.

'Utah to Mass. *or* BUST!'

IT WAS HARD TO BELIEVE HOW FAR FROM HOME THIS LITTLE BOY WAS.

By Barbara Courtright, Laguna Park, Texas

In the early 1960s, my husband, Butch, and I were living in the small town of Kimball, Nebraska, very close to the Wyoming border.

One Friday afternoon, Butch and a friend of his were returning to his floor-covering store from a job in Pine Bluff, Wyoming. They were amazed to see a very young boy riding down the highway on a bicycle and even more amazed to see a sign on his knapsack that read, "Utah to Mass. Or Bust!"

This little boy was a *long* way from home.

After they got back to the store, Butch and his friend went down the street for a cup of coffee and saw the same little boy sitting alone in one of the booths.

Striking up a conversation, they learned of his almost unbelievable story.

His name was Dean, and he and his parents had recently moved from Massachusetts to Utah. He was extremely homesick for his grandparents, friends and the home where he had spent all of his short life.

After begging, pleading and promising to obey each of the many strict rules laid down by his parents, they allowed him to go on his way.

Can you imagine? This young boy, around 13 years old, was on a bicycle, traveling alone all those miles!

Among the rules were: He had to call home each night, and for safety purposes, he carried only a small amount of cash. His father wired money to various towns along the route, enough to last Dean a few days at a time.

Home Away from Home

As Butch and Dean talked in the diner, Butch asked the boy if he would like to spend the night at his house, rather than a motel.

Dean looked them over and asked, "Do you two guys live together?"

Butch explained that he lived with his wife and son Mike, who was about Dean's age. He also explained that since it was Friday night, Mike was allowed to see a movie, adding that perhaps Dean would like to go along.

Dean accepted, with the provision that he first call his parents for permission to stay the night and go to the movie.

When Dean called home, Butch spoke to his parents, giving them complete information about us, including our address and phone number. I believe that he also told them what movie the boys would be seeing.

That settled, we thoroughly enjoyed our short visit with this adventurous little boy.

The next day, we called Sheriff "Hop" Gilster in North Platte, who was our son-in-law's uncle. He said he'd be glad to watch for the young bike rider. Dean was met by a sheriff's posse, which provided safe lodging for the night.

Hop then called a friend in the Grand Island Fire Department; Dean was greeted by a big red fire engine. That friend called ahead to someone in Lincoln, where Dean once again was met at the edge of town.

We had created a domino effect—a support network that remained in place for the balance of Dean's cross-country journey.

A Mini Celebrity

Then we got a card from Dean telling us he was to be a guest on the TV show *I've Got a Secret*. It was exciting to watch as he tried to fool the panel.

The last we heard, Dean was taking a more conventional means of transportation on his return trip to Utah.

Butch and I agreed that Mark Twain, in all his ingenious imagination, couldn't have created a more exciting journey for Huckleberry Finn than the real-life experience of our little friend and traveler, Dean. We'll never forget him.

I wonder where he is today!

If you want children to keep their feet on the ground, put some responsibility on their shoulders.

—Abigail Van Buren

Fun Times In 4-H

Belonging to 4-H was one of the highlights of growing up on a farm in central Wisconsin.

My younger brother, Johnny, and I belonged to the Maple Grove 4-H Club in Wood County. I had so many wonderful experiences during my five years as a member.

I won several honors and a few trips to the Wisconsin State Fair, where I met terrific kids from other clubs.

One of my proudest achievements was the outfit I sewed for my clothing project (shown above right). I won a blue ribbon and placed in the 4-H Style Review at the 1939 Central Wisconsin State Fair.

The dress was lime green, with a coordinating jacket in a darker shade. I wore the green straw hat slightly tilted, in the style of the day.

Johnny (shown with me at right) also excelled in 4-H, winning his share of blue ribbons for gardening and poultry projects.

Most importantly, 4-H taught respect for all and loyalty to our club, community and country.

—*Lucille Schwark*
Dade City, Florida

204

off the beaten base paths

This young ballplayer was caught taking the "Home Sweet Home" message above him literally.

"My brother, Howard Hansen, was taking a much-needed rest in the comfort of our Minnewaukan, North Dakota, home after a day of baseball practice at a local park, in 1962," explains Leslie Hansen of Anoka, Minnesota.

"He went on to become a patrolman with the Minnesota State Patrol and now resides in Hawley with his wife, Diane. Seeing this picture will, I'm sure, bring back a lot of memories for our family."

my own memories